from Worry to Happiness

from Worry to Happiness

Bill W. Flatt

Christian Communications
P.O. Box 150
Nashville, TN 37202

TO

MY FAMILY

My parents

Mr. and Mrs. Benton M. Flatt

whose love, sacrifice, and guidance

have led me toward the Bible

and the Christian way of life

My wife

Louise

and our sons

Steve, Tim, Danny

who enrich my life immeasurably

and contribute greatly to

my mental health

Contents

Preface

This book is an outgrowth of personal reflection, reading, counseling, and preaching. I have searched the Word of God for answers to the perplexities of guilt, worry, fear, insecurity, depression, and grief. I grew up believing the Bible, and I have found no adequate substitute for it. Indeed, what can substitute for the faith, comfort, assurance, love, and hope found in the Bible? What can compare with the love of God, who loved us so much that he gave his Son for us? What can compare with the love of Jesus that led him to the cross for the sins of the world?

The Bible has the solution to our guilt feelings. God offers the forgiveness that we need. Worrying about our sins will not turn the clock back so that we can relive a segment of our lives. But we can obey God's Word, accept his pardon, and begin anew. Other problems can also be resolved. Through trust in God we can conquer our fears and gain eternal security in Christ. The Christian has eternal life; all does not end at the grave. Discouragements are lifted when we realize that God's grace is sufficient for us (II Cor. 12:1–11). The Bible teaches that God created us (Gen. 1–2) and loves us (John 3:16). We are children of God (John 3:5; I John 3: 1–3), and have assurance of salvation because of the lives we live in obedience to him (I John 3:8–20).

The Bible also guides us in our sexuality. God's purpose for us is indicated in his marvelous creation. We are created male and female. Man and woman are designed to become one flesh in marriage. The Bible teaches that the home is part of God's plan for mankind. The home as described in the Bible is to be a place of love, loyalty, work, encouragement, and obedience to God. The home becomes the center from which the Christian relates to the world. Every human being needs such a place where he can be himself, find support, and live without fear of being rejected.

Furthermore, the Bible has the best answer for grief. In our grief God still loves us. He still cares and offers passage to life beyond the grave through his Son, Jesus Christ. "O death, where is thy victory? O death, where is thy sting?" (I Cor. 15:55). The culmination of God's answers to our longings is seen in his promise of life with him forever—where there will be no pain and where God will wipe away every tear from our eyes (Rev. 21:1-8).

I began this study by looking at my own needs and the needs of others. A study of psychology helped me further in this search, since psychology is a study of human thoughts, feelings, and behavior. My frustrations during my ministry in trying to help people with emotional problems led to my graduate studies in psychology and the Bible. This combined study helped me learn more about human problems and their solutions. I believe that God has provided for our needs and that his Word points us to a victorious lifestyle in Jesus. The Bible can help us change our thinking, our behavior, and our feelings. Such changes, however, take time. Cognitive restructuring of the mind goes deeper than mere intellectual assent. We need to learn and internalize vital principles until they become second nature to us. Our behavior must change so drastically that it results in a new lifestyle. Such changes will produce a life of happiness and productivity.

I encourage you to study the Scripture references in this book. If you have serious emotional problems, remember that God loves you, I am concerned about you, and other Christians can help you. You may need a well-trained Christian professional counselor who will strengthen your faith rather than tear it down. A minister of the gospel or a Christian counseling center in your community can assist you with arrangements.

May the Lord bless you. May these chapters help build you up and encourage you to live a happy and useful life.

BILL FLATT

1

How to Handle Guilt Feelings

A serious problem in the church today is the problem of guilt. Many members are not able to deal with feelings of guilt. Some who should feel guilty do not. Others who should be free of guilt's burden suffer because they are unable to accept God's forgiveness. Neither can they forgive themselves for past sins.

We expect criminals to suffer from guilt and to atone for their crimes by paying the penalty demanded by society. Likewise, those rebelling against God's will should feel guilty. But the Christian should turn to God for forgiveness and rid himself of guilt. The problem for many is in accepting God's forgiveness and living free from the burden guilt imposes.

The Bible indicates the need for a clear conscience. Subjective guilt could be defined as a "bothered conscience." All of us need to be free from a bothered conscience. Guilt may also be defined as a subjective feeling of responsibility for wrongdoing, for sin. We must be so concerned about our guilt feelings that we ask God for forgiveness. After we have asked for his forgiveness, feelings of guilt should be set aside.

It is possible to feel too guilty. For example, a certain man had been asked by his wife to pick up some dry cleaning on his way home from the office. He forgot all about it. His wife criticized him for his forgetfulness. He felt extremely guilty and became depressed. He would not speak to anyone for several days after this incident. Perhaps he should have felt some guilt but certainly not as much as he exhibited.

Another man of forty had been passed over for a promotion. He felt that somehow it was his fault. All of his life he had been told that a man could do just about what he wanted to do in life.

Therefore, since he was overlooked, the fault must be his own. He reasoned that there must have been something he could have done to insure his promotion. He went into a period of depression, feeling that his life was not worth living anymore.

The Consequences of Guilt

There are many consequences of guilt feelings. Guilt feelings can cause us to be unproductive and to worry until we are sick. Sin that God has forgiven should not cause us to worry.

Guilt can cause us to do strange things. For example, one person called the police and confessed to a crime he had not committed. His guilt feelings were too strong. There were things in his life that he had done for which he had not received punishment. Therefore, this confession represented a chance to receive punishment he thought he deserved.

Another person's wife brought a book home from a neighbor's house by mistake. This worried her husband, and he accused her of being a thief. Her "theft" bothered his conscience so much that he got up at midnight, returned the book, and confessed his wife's "sin" to the neighbor. His guilt feelings carried over from childhood and caused problems in his marriage.

Guilt can destroy us. We must accept God's forgiveness and accept ourselves as forgiven.

There are many biblical illustrations showing the consequences of guilt. Esau sold his birthright to his brother Jacob for a mess of pottage (Gen. 25:29-34). Later Esau wept and was very bitter. Although he was sorry for what he had done, he did not "find place for repentance" (Heb. 12:14-17). He had "a root of bitterness which defiles and which does not heal." Esau is an example of the destructiveness of guilt.

Saul is another example of destructive guilt feelings. He had many ups and downs in his life. As recorded in I Samuel 17, he tried to kill David. Later, in the next chapter, Saul rewarded David by placing him over his soldiers. However, Saul was infuriated when the women began to sing that Saul had slain his thousands and David his ten thousands (I Sam. 18:9). After Saul threw his spear at David (v. 11), Jehovah departed from him (v. 12). Saul tried to have David killed in war by the Philistines (v. 17). Later he gave David his daughter, Michal, so that she could be a snare to him (v. 21).

Saul tried to destroy David by deception and force and then, because of his guilt, would try to undo what he had done. We see Saul's guilt revealed in I Samuel 19:6 when he told Jonathan that he would not kill David. Later, in verse 10, Saul tried to kill David with a spear and then had eighty-five priests killed because they helped David escape (I Sam. 22:17). Saul was so infuriated that he sought David every day (I Sam. 23:14). David had a chance to kill Saul but instead cut off Saul's skirt in order to prove to him that his life had been in David's hands (I Sam. 24:5). When Saul saw this, he no doubt had guilt feelings as indicated by the fact that he wept (v. 16). Then he said: "Thou art more righteous than I; for thou hast rendered unto me good, whereas I have rendered unto thee evil" (v. 17).

Later, as recorded in I Samuel 26:2, Saul went with 3,000 men to kill David. However, David took Saul's spear and pitcher of water while Saul slept (I Sam. 26:12). In apparent penitence, Saul said, "I have sinned: return, my son David; for I will no more do thee harm, because my life was precious in thine eyes this day: behold, I have played the fool, and have erred exceedingly" (v. 21). God then departed from Saul (I Sam. 28:15). Because of the way Saul lived and the way he handled his guilt feelings, God not only refused to answer him but also took the kingdom from him and gave it to David (I Sam. 28:18). Because of this disobedience Saul was delivered into the hands of the Philistines, with the result that he fell to the ground with all strength gone. He would not eat and was deeply troubled (I Sam. 28:16–21). When he was about to be killed by the Philistines, Saul fell upon his own sword (I Sam. 31:1–6). Three of his sons also died in battle. Saul demonstrates what can happen when guilt is not handled appropriately. Saul's conscience bothered him, but he did not discontinue his mistreatment of David. His guilt led to his destruction.

David demonstrates a good way to handle guilt. He sinned by committing adultery with Bathsheba and then having Uriah, her husband, killed in battle (II Sam. 11–12). These sins distressed David greatly (Ps. 32). Feeling that God's hand was heavy upon him, David turned to God in confession. He ceased to hide his iniquity. He prayed for forgiveness and received it. Then he could say: "Thou art my hiding place; Thou wilt preserve me from trouble; Thou wilt compass me about with songs of deliverance" (Ps. 32:7). He also wrote, "Many sorrows shall be to the wicked; But he that trusteth in Jehovah, lovingkindness shall compass him about. Be glad in Jehovah, and rejoice, ye righteous; And shout for joy, all ye that are upright in heart" (vv. 10–11). Psalm 51 described his joy of salvation because guilt caused him to turn to God for forgiveness.

In Matthew 26 we learn that Judas, one of the twelve apostles, betrayed Jesus for thirty pieces of silver. He kissed Jesus and said, "Hail, Rabbi," in order to identify him for the soldiers. Later Judas had guilt feelings that bothered him so much he returned the money, saying, "I have betrayed innocent blood." But apparently his guilt was not strong enough to cause him to repent. When the authorities were not interested in what he had to say, Judas threw the money down into the sanctuary and went and hanged himself (Matt. 27:5). He had guilt feelings, but they were not handled in the right way. They did not cause him to turn to God.

Peter offers a good example of how to handle guilt. We read in Matthew 26 of Peter declaring that he would never deny Jesus. Later he denies his Lord and with an oath swears that he does not even know Jesus. After this the cock crowed as Jesus had predicted, and Peter "went out and wept bitterly" (Matt. 26:75). Evidently Peter not only felt guilty, but his guilt feelings caused him to turn in repentance to Christ. Just prior to Jesus' ascension into heaven, he indicated his forgiveness of Peter by telling him to feed his sheep (John 21:17). Jesus was Peter's answer. Repentance, forgiveness, and then service will absolve guilt.

The Causes of Guilt

All of these illustrations make us wonder what causes guilt. There are at least two causes. Some things are wrong and thus lead to guilt feelings. If we mistreat someone, we usually feel guilty, as we should. But this guilt, if handled constructively, can lead us to make right what we have done wrong.

James describes sin and lust and what it does to a person in James 1:13–15: "Let no man say when he is tempted, I am tempted of God; for God cannot be tempted with evil, and he himself tempteth no man: but each man is tempted, when he is drawn away by his own lust, and enticed. Then the lust, when it hath conceived, beareth sin: and the sin, when it is full-grown, bringeth forth death." God is not responsible for this type of guilt: we feel guilty because we have sinned. Since sin is destructive and leads to death, we need to turn from it and accept Jesus and his solution. In many cases, a person's guilt feelings can be handled simply by turning from sin and obeying God. If you are in doubt about certain guilt feelings, why not try this: give yourself completely to God and ask his forgiveness.

There is another cause for guilt. It is often the explanation for guilt feelings that are too strong. Some people feel guilty about everything. They apologize for being alive. The cause of such guilt feelings is labeled *conditioning*. We *learn* to feel guilty.

Ivan P. Pavlov, a Russian physiologist, performed the ground-breaking experiment in the study of conditioning. His experiment was conducted in the following manner: Every time Pavlov placed a piece of meat before a dog, he would ring a bell. The dog would salivate whenever the meat was placed before him. After the experiment was repeated a number of times, the dog began to salivate at the ringing of the bell, even though the meat was no longer placed before him. The sound of the bell had been associated with the meat. The dog was conditioned to salivate at the ringing of a bell, although the bell could not be eaten to satisfy his hunger. Many emotions—worry, guilt, fear, discouragement, insecurity—are learned in a similar way.

A few years ago I was driving to Arkansas to conduct a funeral. While going by a certain service station in Marion, Arkansas, I was listening to a tape of my notes on the psychologist B. F. Skinner. Even today when I pass that station, I think of B. F. Skinner. Another example is perhaps more pertinent. Recently I was singing a particular song in church when I noticed that there were tears in my eyes. When I analyzed the reasons for this, I remembered that this song had been sung at the funeral of two of my grandparents. I had been conditioned to be sad at the singing of that song! Tears had come without my having thought about it at all. I had automatically responded with sadness.

Another psychologist who is important to our understanding of the way we learn in early life is Sigmund Freud. In his genetic model Freud taught that we learn everything of significance by the time we are six years old. He believed that after age six a person had no new experiences. Perhaps he overstated his case, but if we are conditioned to feel guilty by that age, we will probably have many guilt feelings later on in life.

One thirty-year-old man said that he felt guilty and depressed. He was a Christian, had done mission work, and in fact was a preacher of the gospel. He was married and a graduate of a Christian college. He had no self-confidence and little self-esteem. He felt insecure and afraid of God. He talked about his inferiority complex and a need to be alone. He felt guilty because he did not like being with people and did not feel secure in his relationship with God. He thought that something was wrong with him. He felt guilty about not going back to the mission field but did not believe he could do any good if he went back because of his fear of associating with people. His church activities were burdensome, and he described himself as being guilt-ridden. Everything he did at church was an ordeal because he did not feel worthy to do what he was doing. He spoke of the long, agonizing depression that he had been in for a number of weeks. He was introverted, unassertive, serious, shy, and tense. Why did he feel so apprehensive and guilty? Why was his self-concept so low? He had a background of being put down. His father had the attitude that children should be seen but not heard. Every time he would try to talk, his father would tell him to shut his mouth. His father was very aloof and, therefore, did not have a close relationship with his children. He had been overly critical of everything the boy did and punished him severely. You can see now what conditioning can do. This man did not feel that he could ever have a good relationship with God. In spite of the fact that he believed, had been baptized, and was a faithful Christian, he was afraid of facing God in judgment. A child that has been beaten often may feel guilty for the rest of his life. He may feel that he is doing something wrong even when he is doing right.

The Bible teaches this principle of conditioning in Proverbs 22:6: "Train up a child in the way he should go, and even when he is old he will not depart from it." The way we treat our children when they are young often determines the way they will feel in the future. If they feel insecure now, they will probably feel insecure in the future. If you do not love them, it will be hard for them to believe that God can love them.

The Answer to Guilt

Guilt is a serious matter. In Numbers 14:18 the writer states, "Jehovah is slow to anger, and abundant in lovingkindness, forgiving iniquity and transgression; and that will by no means clear the guilty..." In James 2:10 the same point on guilt is recorded: "For whosoever shall keep the whole law, and yet stumble in one point, he is become guilty of all." We cannot ignore true guilt.

How can we find the answer to sin and guilt? The answer is in Jesus himself. We read in Isaiah 53:5: "But he was wounded for our transgressions, he was bruised for our iniquities, the chastisement of our peace was upon him; and with his stripes we are healed." In Jeremiah 31:34 we read, "I will forgive their iniquity, and their sin I will remember no more." God does not remember sin that he has forgiven. Why should we?

Paul writes in Titus 2:14 that Jesus "gave himself for us, that he might redeem us from all iniquity, and purify unto himself a people for his own possession, zealous of good works." In Romans 6:4 we learn of the connection between obedience and the death of Christ. Paul writes, "We were buried therefore with him through baptism into death: that like as Christ was raised from the dead through the glory of the Father, so we also might walk in newness of life." It should be a new life free from guilt. In I Peter 1:18–19, Peter admonishes: "Knowing ye were redeemed, not with corruptible things, with silver or gold, from your vain manner of life handed down from your fathers; but with precious blood, as of a lamb without blemish and without spot, even the blood of Christ." In verses 22 and 23 he continues, giving us the other side of the coin, "Seeing ye have purified your souls in your obedience to the truth unto unfeigned love of the brethren, love one another from the heart fervently: having been begotten again, not of corruptible seed, but of incorruptible, through the word of God, which liveth and abideth." Peter teaches that we were redeemed by the blood of Christ and that we purified our souls by our obedience to the truth. It is grace *plus obedience*. Not one or the other but both! This is the way to deal with our guilt feelings. Believe in grace but also believe in obedience.

When we talk about guilt, we are actually facing two problems. One problem is the problem of those who should feel guilty. Those who are burdened with true guilt should turn to God. They have sinned and need God's forgiveness before they can feel right. In Proverbs 28:13 we read, "He that covereth his transgressions shall not prosper; but whoso confesseth and forsaketh them shall obtain mercy." Conversely, many people have been forgiven of their sins and still feel guilty. This is the other problem. There are some who should not feel guilty—they have been forgiven. They should remember God's promise of grace and forgiveness. They should forgive others. They should repent and ask God to forgive them. They should remember that Paul himself was the chief of sinners and was forgiven. We read of this in I Timothy 1:15-16: "Faithful is the saying, and worthy of all acceptation, that Christ Jesus came into the world to save sinners; of whom I am chief: howbeit for this cause I obtained mercy, that in me as chief might Jesus Christ show forth all his longsuffering, for an example of them that should thereafter believe on him unto eternal life." A person who feels guilty should accept God's forgiveness. Then if they remember the sin again, they should thank God for having forgiven them of their sin.

In conclusion, we should be reminded that unresolved guilt can destroy us. It can eat away at us even in our dreams. Have you brought your guilt to Jesus? Do this and live. This is the only way to handle guilt feelings, the only profitable way to live.

QUESTIONS FOR DISCUSSION

1. What is the difference between guilt and guilt feelings?
2. Should we be concerned with both?
3. In Acts 23:1, Paul said that he had lived in all good conscience until that day. What is the relationship between conscience and guilt?
4. Why is it so easy for us to forget about some sins and so hard for us to forget about other sins?
5. How is guilt related to emotional problems?
6. How can parents raise children so that they will feel appropriate guilt but not feel inappropriate guilt?
7. What can faithful Christians do to alleviate guilt feelings?

2

From Worry to Happiness

In Psalm 102 David reflects on his anxiety about the problems of life. He mentions physical problems: his bones cleave to his flesh and he is not able to eat. He worries about his enemies and his relationship with God. Divine indignation bothers him. He worries about his own life—how long he is going to live, whether he will be able to live "the length of his days." He wonders about prisoners and their need to be released from their prisons.

In the latter part of the psalm, he sees that the answer is God. God, he declares, will endure forever: "The children of thy servant shall continue and their seed shall be established before thee."

Psalm 103 begins in praise: "Bless Jehovah, O my soul; and all that is within me, bless his holy name." Throughout this psalm David recognizes that God can help solve both physical and spiritual problems.

What Do You Worry About?

What do you worry about? Everything? Most persons have a long list of worries, and for the majority of us, failure is a part of that list. Because she lost her boyfriend, one young woman of twenty-four thought her world was coming to an end—that she was a total failure. Her desperation led her to take an overdose of sleeping pills. She would have died had she not been found in time and taken to a hospital. She said, "I'm a failure. I'll never be able to get married, and I just can't live this way. I don't want to be alone all my life. I need someone."

We all have goals that we want to achieve. When something happens to prevent this achievement, we worry and often become inactive. We feel out of joint. What, after all, is the use?

When he lost his job, one 55-year-old man was beset with worry. Life was passing him by. Why had he not been successful? He could only blame himself. With this attitude he was unable to overcome and rebound from his setback. Eventually he took his own life.

People worry about marital problems. When conflicts arise between couples, bitterness, resentment, and failure to communicate may result. One woman said, "I am worried. My husband won't talk to me anymore. I'm afraid we are coming apart—I'm worried to death about it."

Others worry about what people think of them. A very upset sixteen-year-old girl told me that people looked down on her because she went to a vocational school. I asked her what she was studying, and she answered that they were just learning how to cook. When I replied, "I really wish I knew how to cook," she was noticeably elated. Why? Her self-concept was low. She thought that others were laughing at her because she was not exactly like them.

Sometimes we worry because no one seems to care. David felt this way. Everyone seemed to be against him. At times, it appears to all of us that no one cares and we bury ourselves in self-pity. This can happen if several "pipes burst in our walls," and problems accumulate. The burden can seem unbearable, and we can easily conclude that "no one cares."

Sometimes we worry about illness. We are fearful that something terrible is going to happen to us or our loved ones. Some such feelings are unavoidable. But if we are continually apprehensive, we are robbed of our Christian joy.

Sometimes we are worried about the future. An eighteen-year-old boy said that he was a failure in life and that he didn't want to keep on living. He was convinced that when he got to college he would flunk out and his father would be very displeased with him. He was so depressed that he decided to take his own life. After a little while, however, he began to see that worry did not help. He began to concentrate on his studies and his grades improved a letter grade in two months.

Problems are not easy to overcome. Rather than laugh at another's problems, we should be very sympathetic. The person may have many burdens: "Bear ye one another's burdens, and so fulfill the law of Christ" (Gal. 6:2). Many little things can pile up in our lives and cause us to worry ourselves sick. As problems accumulate we think, "I might as well give up." When we have a lot of little problems, we may not always know exactly how to deal with them.

Why Do You Worry?

The question of *why* we worry is perhaps more important than the question of *what* we worry about. There are a number of common reasons for worry. First, we worry about the circumstances we face. It is natural to worry when a pipe bursts in a wall; there is nothing unusual or abnormal about such anxiety. But what we do about the problem is more significant than the energy expended in worry.

A young girl came into a social worker's office not too long ago, wanting to discover the cause of her worry. She began talking about the things that had been happening in her life. She had just lost her job, her mother had died a few weeks ago, she had been told by the doctor during the last several days that she might have tuberculosis, and she was expecting a child. And she was puzzled about why she was worried! In her situation most people could not keep from worrying. But even in such circumstances, worry itself will do little good.

A contractor was about to "go crazy" with worry. He had a contract to build a number of houses. When he thought he was getting along well, he struck water and flooded three or four of the houses, almost ruining them. About that time he learned that he had a problem with the title to property on which he had already built ten houses. The bank heard of this and decided to cancel his loan. He had reason to worry in this situation, but such worry, in itself, did not help.

Second, we worry because we have been trained to worry. When parents' lives are rife with worry, so usually are their children's.

Two psychologists, B. F. Skinner and Sigmund Freud, provide help at this point. Freud's teachings on the id, the ego, and the superego are roughly equivalent to the flesh, the self, and the conscience as they are discussed in the Bible. For good mental health, the id, the ego, and the superego must be well-balanced. But our training may lead them to be out of balance. A person's id may be too strong. Controlled completely by the flesh, he may not have any means of restraining himself. If this is true, he will do whatever the flesh suggests that he do. He is trained that way. Without restraints he is going to have great difficulty in life.

A person may have a weak ego. One man continually lamented about how bad everybody was. Nobody was really spiritual. Everybody talked about everybody else. He was bored all the time and was extremely dissatisfied with the world and with everyone in it. Actually, he was extremely weak as a person; he was down on himself—had a very weak self-concept. Projecting his defects to other people, he thought they were the way they were because he was like that. His was a false humility, a "voluntary humility" (Col. 2:18), a self-abasement or self-mortification, which is condemned in the Bible. This can come as a result of our training.

It is also possible for one to have a super superego—one's conscience may be too sensitive. Such a person feels guilty all of the time and about everything. He may confess the same sins to God every week for twenty years or confess that he committed a crime he did not commit.

B. F. Skinner is another psychologist who helps us understand learning. His key concept is *reinforcement*. The Bible also teaches the value of reinforcement: "Train up a child in the way he should go, and when he is old he will not depart from it" (Prov. 22:6). Generally speaking, as the twig is bent, so grows the tree. Skinner demonstrated the value of reinforcement by training pigeons to play Ping-Pong. He placed paddles on their beaks and trained them by using a principle he called operant conditioning. Every time the pigeon did something that Skinner wanted it to do again, it was rewarded with food. Behavior that is rewarded is likely to recur. Skinner simply watched, and when the pigeon moved to the left or right and he wanted it to learn that movement in order to play Ping-Pong, food would drop down to it. He rewarded what he wanted to recur and trained the pigeons to knock the ball back and forth on a table.

Like Skinner's pigeons we can be trained by being reinforced for certain behavior. If we are reinforced for worry, we will probably learn to worry. We will think that somehow it helps the situation if we worry about it. Parents who are afraid of thunder will almost always have children who are also afraid of thunder. If they run and get in the closet when a storm approaches, their children will do the same when they are grown. Why do we worry? Maybe it is because we learned to worry, and we do not know how to learn to stop worrying.

Whether or not we worry is not only dependent on what happens to us but also on what we do with what happens to us. It is a combination of stimulus plus organism plus response. What does the person do with the stimulus, the thunder, for example? This depends on what is inside the person. We can alter our responses, even our emotions: "The same fire that melts the butter hardens the egg." Likewise, the same circumstances that make one person turn against God will cause another person to turn toward God. The same thing can happen to two people. One will worry himself into illness while the other will overcome it. There is a basic difference in the two people, and that difference is extremely important as it relates to worry. Recognizing this fact sometimes helps to overcome worry. Serious problems come to all of us. But even with serious problems, our internal reactions—which we can alter—determine our actions and the outcome of our difficulties.

How Can You Overcome Worry?

Since we worry about many things and for many reasons, we need to learn how to overcome worry. I believe peace of mind is possible even in the worst of circumstances.

One Christian, age forty-five, said that finding out that he had cancer really "threw him for a loop." Filled with serious worries when he first learned of his illness, he was able to work through them. Just after he discovered that he was getting along well with cancer, his doctors revealed to him that he had a heart problem, which would alter his lifestyle considerably. Again, he was very disturbed—down but not out—and again, his answer came from faith. He said, "Knowing that Jesus was in my life helped me to adjust to it. That is the way I got through it."

We all know that there are no easy solutions to serious problems. However, there are strategies, or plans, for attacking worries. One such plan follows:

1. *Analysis.* Analyze the situation that you are worried about. Ask yourself if it will help to worry about it. Usually worry only hinders, frustrates, and petrifies. You should, therefore, not worry about the things you can change nor things you cannot change. You should not worry about what is going to happen nor what is not going to happen. Analyze the situation. You will probably decide that worry in itself is not going to help solve problems. Let worry motivate you to attack the problem that is causing the worry. Set some goals and work toward accomplishing them. When a water pipe bursts, worry alone will not solve the problem of water on the carpets and furniture. You must turn the water off or have it turned off. Analyze the situation and develop a plan of attack. Very serious problems can be approached in a similar way.

2. *Prayer.* Analysis should usually be followed by prayer. God is able to deliver us. We need him every hour; we need him in every plan. Abraham Lincoln once said, "I have often been driven to my knees by the circumstances that I faced." Going to our knees will help because then we have not only our strength but God's strength as well.

3. *Action.* The next step in our plan is to take appropriate action—if action is needed. If there is something that can be done about the problem, then do it. Why worry about it if there is something that can be done to change it? If you are sitting on a tack, why continue to worry about it? Why not get up and pull it out! Indecision prolongs worry. As long as a person is "on the fence," he will continue to worry. It is sometimes difficult to make decisions. But if you will make them, ask God's help to implement them, and then take the appropriate action, you will overcome your worries.

4. *Acceptance.* If prayer and action cannot remove the cause of worry, acceptance is the solution. Some things cannot be changed. That is a hard fact of life for all of us. Even the apostle Paul had to learn to live with his "thorn in the flesh." While it is true that we often do not reach our potential, it is not true that we can do anything we wish to do. We all have limitations. Thus, in some circumstances we need to identify with Job when he said, "Though he slay me, yet will I serve him." This will help us more than the unrealistic statement that asserts: "Any-

thing you want to do, you can do." A person on his deathbed might like to get up and walk off, but he can't do it. This is where acceptance comes in. Accepting what cannot be changed is hard, but it is the only answer.

Paul finally came to see the power of God in the inner man, that he could have peace in spite of the fact that he had physical difficulties. Acceptance is a hard step, but it is sometimes the only step available to troubled people.

A widow recently told me, "You've got to concentrate on what you have, rather than on what you don't have anymore. You've got to make a new life for yourself. Self-pity is a dead-end street." Most of us indulge in self-pity when problems come, but it really is a dead-end street. It doesn't lead anywhere except to a state of emptiness and withdrawal. There had to come a time in this widow's life when acceptance took over. Although the loss of her husband still hurt, she accepted what she could not change. In this way she was able to make a new life for herself.

Paul says in I Corinthians 10:13 that with every temptation there is always a way of escape. God will never give us more trouble than we can bear. We must look for that way of escape; we must look for God's help as we come to accept that which cannot be changed.

5. *Service.* Great strength can come through service. We must look outward. A person who looks only inward will worry himself into sickness. Our first reaction when we are hurt is to look inward. We don't feel like talking to anybody or doing anything. But we must gently force ourselves back into life and begin to associate with others and serve others. The church can help at this point in our attack on worry because the Christian life is a life of service. We should give our bodies as living sacrifices holy and acceptable unto God. This is our spiritual service (Rom. 12:1, 2). Looking out, looking at others—this is excellent therapy for worry. We find ourselves by losing ourselves (Matt. 16:24–26).

6. *Trust.* After all of these steps, we take the final step—trust. When we don't get our way, when things don't go exactly as we want them to go, when things are hard, if we can trust God and really believe that God will take care of us, our trust will help us get over the humps and keep on going. Trust helps smooth out the rough places along life's road. Like Job we hand our prob-

lems to God, trusting that he will take care of them. We still
don't fully understand, but we believe: we trust God.

Several passages in Scripture teach that we should trust God.
Romans 8:28 teaches that all things work together for good to
them that love the Lord and are called according to his purpose.
From Romans 8:31 we learn that God is for us; and since this is
so, who can be against us? You can entrust your life to God and
quit worrying about problems. You are doing everything you
can about it, so why worry?

Jesus himself said that we should not live for money but
rather for him. He says that we ought to consider the lilies of the
field, how they grow: "they toil not, neither do they spin." Yet,
even Solomon in all his glory was not arrayed like one of them.

We worry about food. We worry about what we are going to
wear. We worry about money. We worry about the material
things of life. But worry does not bring solutions. Placing God's
kingdom *first* brings results: then, "all of these things shall be
added unto you" (Matt. 6:24–34).

Examples

Two illustrations from the Bible show two ways of dealing
with worry. The rich young ruler (Mark 10:17–22) came to Jesus
with the question of how to improve himself, how to gain eternal life. Jesus gave him the answer. He was to keep the commandments, which the young man said he had done from the
time of his youth. But in addition to this, Jesus told him to go
and sell what he had and give it to the poor and to come and
follow him in order to have treasures in heaven. That was the
plan. Hearing this, the young man rejected the solution to his
worries and went away sorrowful because he was a man who
had many possessions. Many people make the same mistake.
They are worried and they know the answer, but they do not
accept it.

Another example can be found in I Samuel 1—the example of
Hannah. Hannah was very worried because she had no children. She cried, she did not eat, and her heart was grieved.
Although her husband tried to encourage her, she continued to
be bitter. In the temple she prayed to God and promised him
that if he would give her a child, she would give the child back

to him. By this she meant that her child would be a priest. She was so upset that her lips moved, but her voice was not heard. Hers was a sorrowful spirit, but she poured out her soul before God, and her answer came. Told by Eli, the priest, to go in peace, Hannah began to eat again and was no longer sad. She turned to God and worshiped him. Later, Hannah conceived and bore a son, Samuel. True to her promise to God, Hannah then took her little boy, barely weaned, and gave him to Eli, the temple priest. Hannah's song of thanksgiving is found in I Samuel 2:1–10. She had taken her worries to God, and he had sustained her. She praises God in verse 1 by saying: "My heart exulteth in Jehovah; My horn is exalted in Jehovah; My mouth is enlarged over my enemies; Because I rejoice in thy salvation." She continues, recorded in verse 9, by saying: "He will keep the feet of his holy ones; But the wicked shall be put to silence in darkness; For by strength shall no man prevail." She found the solution to her worries in the strength of God.

The solution for worry comes through analysis, prayer, action, acceptance, service, and trust. Although our lives may be altered permanently by circumstances, they cannot be destroyed if we are able to climb the steps from analysis of the problem to trust in God and his solutions. You have some burdens that only you can bear (Gal. 6:5). You have some burdens that others can help you bear (Gal. 6:2). And you have some burdens that you need to cast on the Lord (Ps. 55:22).

Gal 6:1-5

QUESTIONS FOR DISCUSSION

1. What is the difference between concern and worry?
2. What is the difference between worry and anxiety?
3. What do you worry about?
4. What can you do about it?
5. How do you learn to accept what you cannot change?
6. What scriptures help you to overcome worry?
7. What else have you found helpful?

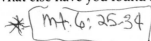
* Mt. 6:25-34

3

How to Deal with Fear

Certain fears are important, and they serve useful functions in our lives. Sometimes being afraid of a car, for example, may prevent us from crossing the street and getting run over. Being afraid of a red-hot stove will cause us not to touch the stove. Being afraid of poison may keep a child from drinking it. So a certain kind of fear is essential. It is commanded in the Bible. Moses instructed Israel to "fear Jehovah, to keep all his statutes and his commandments" (Deut. 6:2). Solomon stated that, "In the fear of Jehovah is strong confidence, and his children shall have a place of refuge. The fear of Jehovah is a fountain of life that one may depart from the snares of death" (Prov. 14:26–27).

A function of fear is to lead us away from evil. People are admonished to "fear God and keep his commandments, for this is the whole duty of man" (Eccles. 12:13). Paul told Timothy to reprove those who sin that the rest also may be in fear (I Tim. 5:20). By faith Noah moved with godly fear and prepared an ark to save his house (Heb. 11:7). The apostle John teaches us to "fear God and give him glory, for the hour of his judgment has come" (Rev. 14:7).

The other side of the coin is that the Bible also teaches us *not* to fear. Paul writes to Timothy, "For God gave us not a spirit of fearfulness; but of power and love and discipline" (II Tim. 1:7). The admonition,"Fear not!" is found numerous times in the Book of Revelation. This is the kind of fear that I am primarily concerned about at this point: neurotic fear and fear instead of courage. Too much fear will destroy our peace of mind. If such fear is a dominant influence in our lives, we will be afraid of almost everything: a ringing phone, a milkman, people, open spaces, God. Fear-ridden people have been conditioned to have too much fear. They are often unproductive and unhappy.

God told Abraham, "Fear not, Abraham, I am thy shield and thy exceeding great reward" (Gen. 15:1). Don't be afraid of the opposition you have. Don't be afraid to carry out your task in life! "Fear not, Abram!" Moses counseled Israel, "Fear ye not, but stand still and see the salvation of Jehovah" (Exod. 14:13). The opposing army was behind them, the sea was in front of them, and Moses told them, "Fear not. Look at what God can do!"

Many situations in our lives are like this. We are between the sea and Pharaoh's army. We need more faith. God is willing to help. In I Chronicles 22:13 we read, "Be strong and of good courage. Fear not, and neither be dismayed." In II Timothy 1:7 we are taught that God did not give us fear.

Excessive fear causes people to function ineffectively and to be unhappy. The Bible's message is designed to take away such fear. I talked to a woman recently who said: "I have no fear whatsoever of death. I am just ready to go anytime the Lord gets ready for me." How wonderful it would be if all of us could face death with such confidence. When the time comes, it may not be that easy. When it is our time to go, we will all probably go through some turmoil. But if we place our faith in God, we can have peace and confidence.

The Effects of Fear

Scripture indicates that fear can hurt us a great deal. In I John 4:18, for example, we read that fear *torments*. We are tormented inside when we are afraid. A person can get to the point where he is scared to think about God. I have seen faithful Christians literally tremble as they thought about the idea of standing before God in judgment. I've seen people who were afraid to go outside of their houses.

The fourth chapter of I John tells us of our relationship with God our Father and of the results of abiding love for Christ our Savior. The more we can really feel this Father–child relationship with God, the more confidence we will have as children of God!

Fear is also connected in some way with bondage. Fear-ridden people are bound up inside and are not really free in the abundant life that Jesus came to give to us. In Romans 8:15 we read, "For ye received not the spirit of bondage again unto fear: but ye received the spirit of adoption, whereby we cry, Abba, Father." Confident Christians feel close to God. He is like an affectionate Father. Such closeness causes us to respect him more, not less. We feel close to him. We don't feel more fearful as we get closer to him but rather have *more assurance* in our hearts.

Fear can stifle initiative. It can cause us to be like the person who was afraid to go outside, afraid to deal with people at all. Fear torments our soul and leads to bondage.

An example of this teaching is found in Numbers 13, where God sent the twelve spies into the Promised Land. They saw that the Promised Land was just as great as God had told them it was. But they came back and said: "Although the land is flowing with milk and honey, we can't take it because there are giants in the land and we are like grasshoppers in comparison to them." They had forgotten that God had said they could take the land because he was going with them. They feared because of the giants in the land. Such fear stifled their initiative; they were paralyzed.

Revelation 21:8 condemns a lifestyle that is dominated by fear. The fearful shall have their part in the "lake that burneth with fire and brimstone."

Two problems are related to fear. One problem leads to crime. Some people don't have enough fear of God, of what is right, of law and order. Because of this lack of fear, they are too aggressive. They may take the law into their own hands, do whatever they want to do. The Bible's message for such a person is to fear God and keep his commandments. On the other extreme, it is possible to have too much fear. Some people are phobic: afraid of people and afraid to do anything. The Bible encourages such people not to be afraid but to believe that God is really with us and that we can do what God wants us to do. It is a matter of striking a balance. The Bible can meet all of our needs. The Bible can have a tremendous effect on our lives.

The Causes of Fear

What causes us to have fear? One could correctly say that the devil is behind it all. He really doesn't want us to have happiness; he doesn't want us to have the peace that God wants us to

have. In the Garden of Eden Satan tempted Adam to disobey
God. Adam's disobedience caused him to be afraid when he
heard God's voice. He was afraid because he had obeyed the
devil. He knew he was not ready to face God.

One might correctly say that a person is responsible for his
own fearfulness. Adam didn't have to do what he did. He chose
to disobey God, and then he had reason to be afraid. One could
also correctly say that fear is caused by circumstances. Do you
remember when Peter, walking on the water, saw the wind and
was afraid (Matt. 14:30)? Contrary winds can cause us to be
afraid if we forget that God is with us.

Another cause of excessive fear is our background. Our experiences can condition us to be afraid. I remember talking to a
woman who was having a great deal of difficulty in her marriage. She was actually afraid of her husband. It seems that she
had developed a fear of men as a little girl. Her father had
frequently come home drunk and beaten her mother. This
legitimate fear of her father was carried over to an irrational fear
of men in general. This made it extremely difficult for this
woman to establish a normal relationship with her husband.

I remember a thirty-year-old man who had a fear of people in
general. If he got into a discussion with a subordinate at work,
he could not hold his own. In every confrontation, he gave in.
He could not argue with anybody. He would either clam up,
walk off, or give in. What was his background? As a child he
never had a chance to talk about his problems or fears. His
father would either shut him up or get a belt and whip him. He
often had stripes on his back because of his father's method of
settling problems in their home. This abuse, which occurred
early in his life, caused him to be intimidated by people as an
adult.

The Cure for Fear

Fear appears to be universal. Therefore, we need to learn to
deal with it in a constructive way. What do we do when fear
torments us? I doubt that we can just forget about it. The more
we try to forget about it, the more we remember it. It is also
virtually impossible to "cheer up" by merely telling yourself to
do so. Excessive fears do not vanish that easily.

After saying these things, I want to mention some helpful approaches to victory over fear. Gaining insight is a first step for many. It helps to have insight into why you feel the way you feel. If you can know that fear is the result of sin in your life, then you know what to do about it. You can turn from your sin and obey God's Word. If you know that your fear comes from severe punishment from your father, you can begin to realize that your problem is not with God or with people in general but with your father. Such insight is a first step toward peace.

Perhaps more important than insight is our faith. Faith can give us peace. The winds and the waves obey Christ's will. The disciples wondered if Jesus cared if they perished. He did care. The wind became still at his word, and the sea was calm. Faith in Jesus is believing that he is going to be with us when the winds are really strong. It sounds too simple, but faith is the solution to fear.

Scripture teaches that faith is essential for coping with fear. We must believe that God is with us, that we are not alone. The person who feels this deeply is well on his way to victory over fear. The psalmist declared his feeling of closeness to God: "Yea though I walk through the valley of the shadow of death, I will fear no evil; for thou art with me" (Ps. 23). The psalmist stated his conviction: "Jehovah is on my side, I will not fear. What can man do unto me?" (Ps. 18:6); "God is my refuge and strength, a very present help in time of trouble" (Ps. 46). Faith is not magic. Even with faith fear will not immediately disappear. But faith is a handle; it is a start.

A lady in her seventies told me that after her son was killed in the service she didn't want to live anymore. In fact, she often thought of taking her own life. She said she would have done so if it had not been for one verse in the Bible. That verse is the one in which Paul says that God's grace is sufficient for him (II Cor. 12:9). She still wasn't completely recovered from her loss, but that verse kept her going. She just kept remembering that God's grace is sufficient for us.

Paul also had problems. His thorn in the flesh remained even though God healed others through him (Acts 28). But Paul knew that God's grace was powerful enough to keep him on his feet.

In Mark 5:35–42 we read the story of a ruler whose daughter had died. This story illustrates the pain and grief that is part of life. This father was afraid. Death was something over which he had no power. Jesus said to him, "Fear not, only believe." Jesus then brought the young girl back to life. You may say that we don't have miracles like this today, and I would agree with you. But I still believe that there is a connection between faith and fear, and that there are a lot of fears that will vanish if our faith is strong. Even the fear of death can be successfully attacked through faith.

When Paul was facing death, he was able to look with confidence toward the end, toward the other side of the valley (II Tim. 4:8). He didn't believe that death was just walking *into* the valley of the shadow, but that the valley led to another place. Death is not a dead-end street: it goes somewhere, to a home with God.

Peter discovered that "in every nation he that feareth him and worketh righteousness is acceptable to him" (Acts 10:35). He later wrote, "Casting all your anxiety upon him, because he careth for you" (I Peter 5:7). Jesus said, "Let not your heart be troubled, believe in God, believe also in me" (John 14:1). Belief will help diminish trouble.

Two of my favorite verses along these lines are II Timothy 1:7 and I John 4:18. These verses say that God does not give us fear but that perfect love casts out fear. He wants us to have confidence. He wants us to believe. Love leads to a healthy reverence for God but not fear. We may never completely reach this point of love's perfection in this life, but such levels of spiritual maturity can be our goal. If love is completely perfected in our hearts, fear will disappear.

Peter wrote, "And fear not their fear, neither be troubled" (I Peter 3:13–14). "Their fear" is the fear of the world. The world has many things which may cause fear. Christians may have some fears, but they are not the *same* fears as are the fears of the world. Don't be troubled as the world is troubled. The Christian should have peace within. Jesus said, "It is I; be not afraid" (John 6:20).

I once read about a rich man who asked two artists to depict peace. One artist painted a beautiful beach, with beautiful trees in the background, and water that was very peaceful, with grass all around and cows grazing in the distance.

The other artist had a different idea of peace. He painted a high waterfall with water roaring down the falls and a tremendous wind blowing the trees back and forth. Up in one of the trees, as it was swaying to and fro, was a bird's nest. In the nest was a bird sitting contentedly on her eggs. This was peace in the midst of turmoil. The artist was saying that there are winds in the world, but in spite of them, with God's help, we can survive. We can cope. We can stand on our own as people of faith.

When our youngest son, Danny, was in junior high school, his goal was to throw the shot sixty feet, which is quite a toss as you may know. No one in Memphis had ever thrown the shot that far. He went out to Halle Stadium one day, took a tape, measured off sixty feet, and drove a stick into the ground at that point. All that week he thought about hitting that stick. Not only did he want to put the shot sixty feet, he wanted to hit that stick. On the day of the meet, Danny threw that shot into the air, and it came down right on top of the stick. He has the broken stick in his room. To me that illustrates what believing can do. We don't have to believe in present-day miracles to believe that faith can do a lot for us in our lives. I believe that faith can help us to overcome fear.

The Bible illustrates the power of faith over fear. Job said that the thing he greatly feared had come upon him (Job 3:25). The negative report of ten spies caused Israel to delay their entrance into the Promised Land (Num. 13). But, on the positive side, faith moves mountains (Mark 10:23) and trees (Luke 17:6)—even the faith of a grain of mustard seed (Matt. 17:20) can do great things. Real faith moves mountains of fears from blocking our progress. Jesus leaned into his fears in the Garden and overcame them (Matt. 26–27). This is indeed a noble example for us to follow. God wants us to control our fears with his help and to serve him with gladness. We can confidently declare, "I can do all things through Christ who strengthens me" (Phil. 4:13).

QUESTIONS FOR DISCUSSION

1. What is the difference between proper fear and improper fear?
2. Have you ever been too fearful? How did such fear affect you?
3. Which is a more effective motivator, love or fear?
4. If perfect love casts out fear (I John 4:18), how perfect is your love?

5. What implications are there in this chapter for child-rearing practices?
6. What fears are hampering your Christian life?
7. Share some ideas on how to overcome them.

4

How to Handle Discouragement

The apostle Paul, one of the greatest apostles in the church, was often discouraged. In II Corinthians 11:22–12:10 he discusses discouraging struggles in his life. His break from his early religion was not always appreciated. The same could be said for his Christian ministry: he was thrown into prison, beaten with rods, stoned, and shipwrecked. He had been hungry and thirsty, cold and naked. And he experienced inward anxiety for all the churches. In addition, he was given a thorn in the flesh which God would not remove. God's answer to Paul was: "My grace is sufficient for thee; for my power is made perfect in weakness" (II Cor. 12:9). Paul concluded: "Most gladly therefore will I rather glory in my weaknesses, that the power of Christ may rest upon me. Wherefore I take pleasure in weaknesses, in injuries, in necessities, in persecution, in distresses, for Christ's sake: for when I am weak, then am I strong" (II Cor. 12:9–10).

Certainly none of us would deny the reality of discouragement. All of us, at times, get discouraged. A young person may think he is doing so poorly in school that he should quit. A homemaker may feel discouraged because she can't keep the house clean. A father may think that his children don't appreciate anything he does for them, that he should quit his job, that he is a failure. Even leaders in the church may think, "I work all the time, but nobody seems to appreciate what I am doing." Bible school teachers may think, "I study every week, and no one seems to care about what I am doing." Personal workers may say, "I have already visited that person six times and nothing has worked. I'm discouraged. I don't see much value in continuing to try." An entire family may, at times, think that they are not appreciated or needed. Discouragement can defeat us in every worthwhile goal we have in life. At one time or another discouragement comes to each of us.

The Causes of Discouragement

What causes people to get discouraged? It is often difficult to pinpoint the cause of anything. Yet we all know there are causes of discouragement. Often discouragement begins in the home. Some are easily discouraged because of the experiences they had as children. A wife said that her husband could be extremely encouraged and enthusiastic; but she could disagree with him about one thing, and he would get so discouraged that he would be moody—down and depressed—for three or four weeks. He explained that he had a rough childhood and was shunted from one place to another after his parents gave him up. Discouragement may stem from lack of love in the home. A friend of mine has an unusual bumper sticker on his car. It reads, "Have you hugged your children today?" High opinions and low opinions of self begin in the home. Children who are not loved are easily turned from their goals in life. They feel unworthy of pursuing worthy goals.

Sometimes standards are too high in the home. The child does his best, but it is never quite good enough. If he comes home with a B, the parents will say, "Why didn't you make an A?" One boy's father came to one of his son's football games. The boy was thrilled that he made a tackle behind the scrimmage line, but the father remarked to his son after the game: "Why did you hit him so high?" Such children never have really satisfying experiences because the standards set for them are too high.

Sometimes the lack of interaction between parents and children can cause children to develop in such a way as to be easily discouraged. Interaction means participation, talking things out with each other. You neither clam up nor blow up at conflicts in the home. Such interaction teaches children how to cope with setbacks.

Unfavorable comparisons of brothers and sisters can cause difficulties in the home. Children who are put down by such comparisons do not develop adequate self-esteem. They are easily discouraged. Parents should avoid such comparisons, especially if one child has more ability than another child. Parents should never say, "You did not do as well as your sister did. What's wrong with you?" Perhaps the child is trying and just can't do as well as the other children did. Each child should be evaluated in terms of what he or she can do rather than in terms of what brothers and sisters can do. In fact, children sometimes hate each other because their parents turned them against each other by unfavorable comparisons. Each child has individual worth in the sight of God.

Schools may also contribute to the problem. Teachers can do some of the same things that parents do to discourage and depress children. They can refuse to be satisfied with the child's work. They can be overly critical.

Sin sometimes causes discouragement. All have sinned (Rom. 3:23), but not all have turned to God for forgiveness. God is able to help us work through our problems. He will lead us through Christ and his Word. Being born again won't solve every problem, but it will help toward solutions of the primary problems of mankind. God's presence in our lives is encouraging and strengthening.

Sometimes we Christians are discouraged because we don't really enjoy the blessings we have in Jesus Christ. I heard a story a number of years ago that illustrates this point very well. A man bought a ticket to travel on a ship to Germany. He had barely enough money to buy his ticket. Knowing that he didn't have enough money left to buy meals at the restaurant on the ship, he saved a little more money and bought some cheese and crackers and carried them with him on the ship. For several days his meals consisted of cheese and crackers. Then one day someone commented, "Say, I haven't seen you down at the ship's restaurant. Where have you been? Why haven't you been coming and eating with us?" He explained that he was broke, had been eating cheese and crackers, and that they shouldn't worry about him. To his surprise, he was told that the ticket he had bought included the price of meals on the ship. He could have been eating delicious meals from the restaurant all along. The point is that we often do not enjoy the spiritual benefits of being in Christ. The fact of our salvation should give us a good feeling inside. The blood of Jesus bought our salvation and provides us with joy and peace. God provides the way of escape from our burdens to a life of contentment.

The Cure for Discouragement

More important perhaps than the causes of discouragement is the cure. How do we deal with discouragement? First of all, we must encourage ourselves. We have to do what we can to help ourselves; we must be determined not to be turned back by every obstacle that we face.

In the spring of 1977, John Dent was playing tennis in Memphis. He was behind in one particular game when he made an excellent shot and nobody applauded. You know what Dent did? Looking back toward where we were sitting, he applauded himself. He seemed to be saying, "If you are not going to do it, I will." Sometimes we need to say, "I can do all things through Christ who strengthens me" (Phil. 4:13).

We must not withdraw from the problems we have. There is no way we can deal with them if we do that. We ought to attack our problems one at a time and find solutions. Take this approach even if you have twenty things to do. This gives you a starting point. You are answering a letter, someone knocks on the door, the phone rings, plans must be finalized for next week's trip—everything calls for attention at once. But don't think about everything at once. If you do, you'll get so discouraged you may want to quit. Do one thing at a time. Amazingly, if you will work on tasks this way, you will accomplish great things. You are helping yourself out of the situation rather than becoming frightened and stymied by discouragement.

We need to allow other people to encourage us. Sometimes we can be in a crowd and still be alone. We are keeping people out of our lives. We won't let people help us. There are many people who care—people at church, people in the community. If we will let them come into our lives, they can help us overcome many difficulties. Someone cares about you. I know that this is true in a Christian community. Somebody cares. They are not trying to manipulate you or to use you. Open up and share yourself and be enriched by the friendship of other people.

We should also allow God to encourage us. He helps us defeat discouragement. The Bible is packed with passages that speak of

God's encouragement. For example, the Bible teaches that God cleanses us from our sins. That news is encouraging to me. I believe that God has cleansed me from my sins. Every sin that I have ever committed has been taken away in the blood of the Lamb. That is one of the most encouraging thoughts that I have ever had.

In I Corinthians 6:9–11 we read about some people who were unrighteous. They were murderers, drunkards, and adulterers. But they had been washed, sanctified, and justified in the name of the Lord Jesus Christ. When we come to Christ, we can believe that the blood of Jesus Christ takes our sins away (Gal. 3:26–27; Acts 2:38; I Peter 3:21). Christians need this encouragement. To believe that we are all right with God is encouraging! Such faith lifts us out of depression and discouragement.

John wrote, "But if we walk in the light, as he is in the light, we have fellowship one with another, and the blood of Jesus his Son cleanseth us from all sin" (I John 1:7). The word *cleanseth* in this verse means "keeps on cleaning us." John is writing to Christians. God not only cleanses us of our sins when we are baptized into Christ, but he continues to cleanse us of our sins as we walk in the light, as he is in the light.

Scripture teaches that God comforts us. In II Corinthians 1:3–5 Paul writes of his sufferings. The sufferings were great, but the comfort was greater. Paul knew that God is the God of all mercy and comfort. He helps us in many ways—through teaching, faith, mercy, love, as well as in ways beyond our understanding.

Scripture also tells us that God encourages us by giving us strength. Isaiah 40:28–31 tells us of how God gives his strength to his people. God strengthens us in the inner person. "Have you not known? Have you not heard? The Lord is the everlasting God, the Creator of the ends of the earth. He does not faint or grow weary, his understanding is unsearchable. He gives power to the faint, and to him who has no might he increases his strength. Even youths shall be faint and be weary, and young men shall fall exhausted. But they who wait for the Lord shall renew their strength, they shall mount up with wings like eagles, they shall run and not be weary, they shall walk, and not faint." Strength comes to the person who waits on the Lord. God encourages us in so many ways. God's power works in the inner person when we let him into our lives.

God also encourages us by giving us hope. In I Peter 1:3–4 we read these words, "Blessed be the God and Father of our Lord Jesus Christ, who according to his great mercy, begat us again unto a living hope by the resurrection of Jesus Christ from the dead, unto an inheritance incorruptible, and undefiled, and that fadeth not away, reserved in heaven for you." In Christ we have hope that there is life beyond the grave, that there is fellowship with God beyond the grave, that difficult times are going to get better, and that we will eventually live with God eternally.

A verse that summarizes the encouragement that God can give us is found in Philippians 4:19. It teaches that God provides for all of our needs. Paul wrote, "My God shall supply your every need according to his riches in glory in Jesus Christ." Such faith encourages and strengthens. He will provide. He will make it possible for us to have what we really need. God is at the center of the cure for discouragement.

Examples

Here are a few examples of how some people have dealt with discouragement. A certain woman who now lives in Kentucky was born without arms. She is an amazing person. She has learned to drive a car, dial a telephone, and even peel potatoes. She is the mother of two children. She did not drift into self-pity because of these difficulties but adjusted to them.

The Bible also records some interesting examples. Paul's road in life was rough. He was in jail when he wrote the Book of Philippians, yet he speaks of rejoicing in the Lord. He says that the peace of God passes all understanding (4:4–9). He was able to sing while in jail (Acts 16). He sang songs at midnight. Over and over again he had something that caused him to be happy even when circumstances seemed to be working against him. I believe that he knew the secret of Christianity. Everything doesn't have to be going exactly right for you to feel right inside. This is not easy to do. It is a difficult challenge—to sing songs in the night, to believe, and to know that God's grace is sufficient.

In I Kings 17–19 we read of a man named Elijah, one of God's greatest prophets. Elijah was a tremendous man. He prayed that God would come down and take his sacrifice. The 450 prophets of Baal had failed to arouse their god, but Elijah was successful.

God answered, and Queen Jezebel threatened to kill Elijah before the end of the next day. Elijah ran away. He withdrew from his problem and became very depressed. He even wanted God to take his life. He was faithful to God but nobody listened to him. He thought that he was the only one left in Israel who had not bowed to Baal. He gave up; he wanted to die.

God encouraged Elijah by telling him that others still cared, that there were 7,000 whose knees had not bowed to Baal. For the discouraged God's message to Elijah is still helpful: there is love, there is fellowship, and there is a task. God told Elijah, "Go appoint Hazael as king over Syria. Get out of this cave. What are you doing here all by yourself? Go appoint Hazael as king over Syria, appoint Jehu as king over Israel, and appoint Elisha as prophet in your place." Elijah was encouraged by the voice of God. When he performed his task he felt better. There is always a task in front of us. There are always goals. Think of those goals and don't let little things or big things keep you from striving for worthy goals in your life.

Another man was often called a failure: he had a difficult childhood and less than one year of formal schooling. He failed in business. His fiancee died. Only one of four sons lived past the age of eighteen. He was defeated for congress at least twice and for the senate once. He was defeated for vice-president in 1856 and defeated for the senate in 1858, but was elected president in 1860. Abraham Lincoln was no failure. Why? He did not give up. He was persistent!

Discouragement can cause us to be defeated no matter what our goal is, but persistence, with faith in God, can help us to achieve our goals.

QUESTIONS FOR DISCUSSION

1. What is the difference between discouragement and depression?
2. What triggers depression in you?
3. How can moods be altered?
4. How can we help each other when we are discouraged?
5. What scriptures are especially encouraging to you?
6. Is it sinful to be depressed?
7. Is God concerned about depression?

5

Changing Insecurity into Security

We are all interested in feeling secure. So were many characters mentioned in the Bible. David knew that his security was in God. In Psalm 16:8 he says, "I shall not be moved." He closes the psalm by writing, "Thou wilt show me the path of life. In thy presence is fulness of joy. At thy right hand there are pleasures for evermore." Setting his feet on solid ground and having security was possible with God's help. This attitude is also expressed in Psalm 40:1-3: "I waited patiently for the Lord and he inclined unto me and heard my cry. He brought me up also out of the horrible pit, out of the miry clay, and set my feet upon a rock and established my goings. He hath put a new song in my mouth, even praise unto our God. Many shall see it and fear and shall trust in the Lord." The writer was standing on solid ground. His security was in the Lord.

The Consequences of Insecurity

We all know the shaky feeling of insecurity. At one time or another it has bothered each of us. Others are bothered by it constantly. I remember meeting a man who had just completed his Ph.D. degree from a large university. He had a nice family, a new car, and a beautiful home. But he was extremely insecure when he was in a classroom. He would back down on any disagreement with a student. He was unusually insecure, and this affected everything he did.

I also remember a young lady who seemingly had everything going for her in life. She was single, popular, attractive, and appeared to be very happy. But, in fact, she was extremely unhappy. As she told her story, she revealed that she had always felt insecure. As a child she had never enjoyed a good relationship with her parents. She had always felt that they were aloof and was unable to feel close to them. She had always wanted her father's approval but never received it. As an adult, trying hard to have a good relationship with men, she would invariably do whatever they asked her to do. This led to promiscuousness, and when one of her boyfriends told her that he did not want to see her anymore, she took an overdose of pills and was taken to a hospital. Later she was able to see that her insecure feelings had led to an exaggerated need for approval from men and had caused her to attempt suicide.

One young wife was extremely jealous of her husband. She felt he didn't love her because he sometimes walked alone in the woods for an hour or more. "If he wanted to be away from me," she cried, "he shouldn't have gotten married." Her feelings of insecurity could be traced to her childhood when her father was always threatening to leave her mother. You can imagine the effect this would have on a small girl who loved her father. Her insecurity as a wife caused her to be extremely jealous of her husband, often accusing him of doing things he did not do.

Another woman, age thirty-nine and mother of nine children, was having difficulty with her husband. He often told her that she was nothing. "You are just a nobody," he would say. When she told him that this hurt her feelings, he replied that it couldn't possibly hurt her feelings, because "you can't hurt the feelings of a nothing." Can you imagine hearing that for nineteen years? How would this make you feel? She felt trapped, she cried, she was afraid.

Such feelings of being trapped and insecure are common. So are feelings of spiritual insecurity. Sometimes Christians do not really feel secure in their relationship with God. They are unsure of their salvation. While we should not feel haughty about it, we should be able to affirm our relationship with our Father in heaven. By the blood of Jesus, we are saved. We should be able to feel some sense of inner security because of such salvation: "Blessed assurance, Jesus is mine."

The Causes of Insecurity

Why do people feel insecure? What are the causes? There are physical causes, emotional causes, and spiritual causes. When personal needs are unmet, we feel insecure. Abraham Maslow has organized human needs into a triangular hierarchy. Physical needs are at the bottom of this triangle, emotional needs come next, and spiritual needs are at the top. The reason for this arrangement is that we usually satisfy physical needs before emotional needs, and emotional needs before spiritual needs.

Who can ignore physical needs such as air, food, and water? These needs cry out for fulfillment. Emotional and spiritual needs are not as urgently felt by most people. Thus, if a man is starving and you say to him, "I love you and want to save your soul," he is not going to listen. His physical needs cry out for help.

Maslow's list of emotional needs includes the need for understanding, for acceptance, for recognition, and for love. Such needs cannot be met either by overprotective parents who never encourage their children to stand up and take responsibility or by parents who are too critical of their children, never giving them recognition or praise for anything they do. Most of us know this fact: it is possible to emotionally starve people, to prevent them from having any successful experiences. An emotionally-starved person will find it difficult to feel secure before God. Since he is our Father in heaven, we may expect little of him if we have received little from our father on earth. One man whose father often beat him with a stick when he was a boy imagined that God was "a man with a stick." A father who is what he ought to be provides a good illustration of God. When a child grows up with rejection in the home, he is conditioned to feel insecure. He does not believe that he has a solid rock on which to stand.

Did you ever see a mule pulling a molasses mill? He walks around and around all day long. A neighbor of mine had such a mule. The mule pulled the mill for most of his life and was then turned out to pasture to roam and graze wherever he chose. Do you know what the mule did? He went around and around out in the pasture. Even when he grazed, he would go around in a circle.

I remember talking to a lady about her fear of thunder. She said she was not going to teach her children that fear. I asked what she did with the children when it thundered. She said, "Well, I protect my children. I take them in the closet with me." Can you imagine what they were learning? They learned to be afraid of thunder!

Physical illnesses, injuries, or inadequacies as children can sometimes cause us to feel insecure as adults. Adjustment to such circumstances is sometimes difficult though not impossible. The inward reaction in such cases may be a feeling of insecurity. In order to be self-confident, a person must learn to accept himself.

There are also some spiritual problems that lead to feelings of insecurity. We realize that we have all sinned and have fallen short of the glory of God (Rom. 3:23). We know also that sin separates us from God (Isa. 59:1–2). Therefore, it is appropriate that a person should have some feeling of insecurity because of sin in his life. He feels as though he is not right with God because he isn't. He needs to adequately deal with the sin in his life in order to feel right before God (Acts 8:26–39).

The Cure for Insecurity

There is a solution for feelings of insecurity. It is not to be found in places where many people look for it. Wickedness, for example, is not a solution. In Isaiah 47 the people tried unsuccessfully to find security in wickedness. The sinful Babylonians had placed their security in themselves and in pleasures. They had committed many sins for which they could not atone. There was no one who could save them from the flames of the fire. Only God can give us security. Only God can atone for what is wrong in our lives and place our feet upon a rock.

Money is another popular, yet inadequate, solution for feelings of insecurity. Money in itself cannot even cause feelings of temporal security, to say nothing of eternal security. Money cannot erase early conditioning, and it cannot buy spiritual treasures. In Luke 12 Jesus tells us about a rich farmer who said he was going to build bigger barns, fill them with his wealth, and say, "Soul, take thine ease... Everything is o.k." His plan failed miserably. That night his soul was required of him.

In I Timothy 6:10 we read that love of money is the root of all kinds of evil. But godliness with contentment is a great virtue, for we brought nothing into this world and certainly we can take nothing out of it. When people strive to find security in the wealth of this earth, their hearts are broken because they are seeking security in the wrong place.

In Ecclesiastes 2 Solomon tells us of the futility of striving for happiness and security in earthly pleasures alone. With all the wealth in the world at his hand, Solomon could not find true happiness. He concludes in verses 10 and 11: "And whatsoever mine eyes desired, I kept not from them. I withheld not my heart from any joy; for my heart rejoiced in all my labor; and this was my portion from all my labor. Then I looked on all the works that my hands had wrought and all the labor that I had labored to do. And, behold, all was vanity." All of this was vanity and vexation of spirit, and there was no profit under the sun. It was like he was striving after the wind. Solomon was like the movie star who successfully seeks after fame and then is not satisfied, who is still empty inside because he or she is seeking security in the wrong place.

The Bible teaches that the only real security that we will ever have in this world is through Jesus Christ our Lord. Death is evidence for this conclusion. Eternal hope reaches beyond the grave to security in fellowship with God. Our refuge and joy is in the Lord. The Lord can place our feet upon a rock, pull us up out of the pit, and make us feel that our only security is in the Lord. This is a very meaningful concept to many who are facing death: to feel right with the Lord is everything to them at that point. Real security is found only in God. Isaiah reflects such faith by writing, "Thou wilt keep him in perfect peace, whose mind is stayed on thee, because he trusteth in thee" (Isa. 26:3). So Jesus tells us, "Seek ye first his kingdom, and his righteousness, and all these things shall be added unto you" (Matt. 6:33).

We read of how important love is as we think of security. Of faith, hope, and love, the greatest of these is love (I Cor. 13). God loves us (I John 4), we love God (I John 5:3), and we love each other (John 13:34–35; Rom. 12:9–10; I Peter 1:22).

Grace is extremely important for security. We have peace through faith, because faith leads us to Jesus and an obedient life in Jesus (Rom. 5:1–2). We have grace through which we can feel secure. When God is for us, who can be against us (Rom.

8:31–39)? Therefore, the faithful child of God should feel a blessed assurance in his heart. We are more than conquerors
through him that loved us. Paul was persuaded that none of the
things of which people are usually afraid, whether life or death,
principalities or powers, demons or spiritual powers, would be
able to separate us from the love of God in Christ Jesus our
Lord. Do you feel that strength and security? The same power
that raised Jesus Christ from the dead is at work in us. God is
the author of security and peace (Eph. 1:19–20; Phil. 4:4–9).

Faith is necessary for victory over insecurity: "This is the
victory that overcometh the world, even our faith" (I John 5:4).
This way of faith is the way of overcoming all of our obstacles.
Eternal security is absolutely essential if we are to have any real
feeling of stability. There is no other hope, because death, without God, is king. Faith in God can do more than can either
wealth or fame to give a person a feeling of internal security. If,
for example, a person feels extremely insecure inside, you can
give him a million dollars, and he will still feel insecure. You
could elect him governor of a state, and this would not change
his inward inclinations. But if he comes to have a real faith in
God, he will feel an inner confidence and security.

Jesus said, "If a man love me, he will keep my word, and my
father will love him, and we will come unto him and make our
abode with him" (John 14:23). This is fellowship. It should give
us a feeling of strength and security. As long as God is walking
with us, we can be certain that our feet are on a solid rock! The
key to all of this is surrender to God. We must know inwardly
that we are not holding out on him. Jesus said, "If any man will
save his life, he will lose it. But if any man shall lose his life for
my sake, he will find it. If a man shall gain the whole world and
lose his soul, what does it profit?" (Matt. 16:24–26).

I recently read a lovely poem by Helen Steiner Rice, called
"Climb Until Your Dream Comes True." The importance of faith
and security are reflected in this poem:

> Often your tasks will be many, and more than you think you can
>   do,
> Often the road will be rugged, and the hills insurmountable too,
> But always remember, the hills ahead are never as steep as they
>   seem,
> With faith in your heart, start upward and climb til you reach
>   your dream.

For nothing in life that is worthy, is too hard to achieve
If you have the courage to try it, and you have the faith to believe.
For faith is a force that is greater than knowledge, or power, or skill
And many defeats turn in triumph, if you trust in God's wisdom and will.
For faith is a mover of mountains. There is nothing that God cannot do
So start out today with faith in your heart, and climb until your dream comes true.

Examples

Job is a good illustration of one who found security in God. His ten children were taken away from him, his wife turned against him, and he became very ill. Yet his attitude was, "I will still trust in God." He believed that God was his security. His future and his security were not dependent on wealth or health or even on precious human relationships. Job said, "Naked came I out of my mother's womb, and naked shall I return thither: Jehovah gave, and Jehovah hath taken away; blessed be the name of Jehovah" (Job 1:21).

Solomon sought security in many places: wealth, pleasure, fame. He concludes his short book, Ecclesiastes, by saying, "This is the end of the matter; all hath been heard: Fear God and keep his commandments; for this is the whole duty of man. For God will bring every work into judgment, with every hidden thing, whether it be good, or whether it be evil." Solomon knew that only God could provide a lasting and meaningful sense of security.

There are difficulties in life, but overcoming these difficulties can make us stronger, bring us closer to God, and give us a feeling of security. Toward the end of his life, Paul, having been through many difficulties, was able to face death with confidence because he trusted in God. Paul believed that a "crown of righteousness" would be given to him and to all faithful Christians (II Tim. 4:8). God can bring us eternal security through Jesus Christ, his Son. Grace, faith, and obedience lead to this goal (Rom. 5:1; Eph. 2:8-9; Acts 2:22-38). Whatever it costs, eternal security will be worth much more than the price. Thank God! He has given us the victory through Jesus Christ our Lord. He has placed our feet on solid rock.

QUESTIONS FOR DISCUSSION

1. Is it possible to be secure in this life?
2. How do feelings of insecurity affect your life?
3. What implications do you see in this chapter for child-rearing practices?
4. Does one ever outgrow early feelings of insecurity?
5. How?
6. What kind of preaching would help you deal with your feelings of insecurity?
7. Is it possible to feel too confident, too sure of yourself, too secure?

The Integrity of the Person

When Neil Armstrong stepped onto the moon, his first words were, "One small step for man; one giant leap for mankind." Indeed, it was a giant leap technologically for mankind. Back on the earth, however, things are moving more slowly. Steps need to be taken to bring people closer together. Thus, I would like to propose one giant leap forward—the recognition of the worth of each person.

To suggest the importance of taking this leap is not to say that other steps are unimportant, that other advances are not needed. Rather, it suggests that advances could be made in the area of interpersonal relationships and for the gospel of Christ if we would first of all take this one leap forward—if we would develop the attitude that each person has individual integrity because he is a person, that he has intrinsic worth as a person because he was created in the image of God.

The early Restoration leaders saw the importance of concentrating on one thing at a time. For example, they suggested that the acceptance of the Bible as the only authority in matters of religion would be a giant leap forward. Indeed it was and is. But other leaps were needed then, and they are needed today.

The Need for the "Leap"

There is a tremendous need in our world today for this leap forward—this acceptance of every individual as a person of value.

Much of the inhumanity in the world has been brought about

by people who say they believe in God. This is true from the Crusades through the Inquisition and even today.

In 1969 the meeting of the U.S. Congress on Evangelism, composed of 5,000 delegates from 95 denominations, indicted Christians by saying that they often preached love for God and practiced hate for people. There is at least some truth in their allegations. Compassion has often been lacking. We must not only be concerned about small things such as the use of tobacco, but also about big things such as war, peace, and poverty. We must not only speak of Christian commitment but also put it into practice by treating people with kindness. Some in this conference, including Senator Mark Hatfield, said that they often get letters from people who speak of their Christian commitment and then take off on a tirade, usually on petty issues. They sometimes use profane language and then end by signing the letter, "Sincerely in Christ." Senator Hatfield stated that he learned not to discriminate against people by studying Acts 10—Peter's vision of unclean beasts—and praying about it.

A black counselor said that she had been turned down for many jobs by clubs and other groups because of her color. Because of this she marched for civil rights. While she was marching, she said, many Bible-believing people spat in her face. "You people talk a lot about God, and the love of Jesus," she said, "but you keep me from buying a house in your neighborhood, you keep me from getting a job, you keep me out of the Bridge Club, just because I am black. I have been unable at times in my life to get a room in a hotel because I am black. How do you think this makes me feel? Why don't you talk a little less about love of God and Jesus and practice it a little more?"

Sometimes in the church we talk about our love for people and then turn against them. People of different races are not welcome in some congregations. We write about loving people and then neglect their needs. This is another way of saying, "Be ye warmed and filled, notwithstanding ye give them not the things needful to the body."

Examples from Scripture

The Bible certainly teaches the worth of all persons. Each person is of value because he or she is made in the image of God

(Gen. 1:27). God breathed into man's nostrils the breath of life and he became a living soul (Gen. 2:7). Man is made a little lower than the angels (Ps. 8:3–5). God not only clothed the lilies of the field but is concerned that the needs of his people be met (Matt. 6:25–30). Jesus praised the good Samaritan for helping the man who had been robbed and beaten. The priest and the Levite, who left the man lying on the side of the road, were concerned about serving God in their own way but were not concerned about serving God in God's way. They did not care enough about people to help them (Luke 10:30–37). Jesus commended the Samaritan as a model neighbor. He showed mercy, and Jesus said, "Go and do thou likewise."

Doing unto others as we would have them do unto us is the heart of the religion of Jesus (Matt. 7:12). This is loving God with all the heart, soul, and mind, and loving one's neighbor as oneself (Matt. 22:37–39). The kind of love that God demands leads to interaction with people. This is the badge of true discipleship (John 13:35). The Bible certainly does not distinguish between loving God and loving people. We cannot love God unless we love our brother (I John 4:20). It is not an either/or proposition: loving God means meeting eternal and temporal needs of people.

I'm OK, You're OK

Jesus said that we are to love our neighbor as ourselves. This indicates that we must have a positive attitude toward ourselves. In fact, it may be impossible to love our neighbor if we do not have proper regard for ourselves. A book entitled *I'm OK— You're OK* by Thomas A. Harris describes four attitudes one might have toward himself and others.

1. *I'm not OK—You're OK.* Harris suggests that a baby has this attitude because he is small and helpless; whereas, adults are large, helpful, and strong. The baby wants to get the adult's attention and approval. Harris further states that if we keep this attitude as adults we may live with the feeling that all things will be all right *if,* or that everything will be all right *when.* This kind of person may try extremely hard to gain the approval of others, especially approval from important people, may withdraw from life, since it is too painful for such a person to be around OK

people. This person's search for happiness is futile because his basic life position has not changed. "No matter what I do, I'm still not OK."

2. *I'm not OK—You're not OK*. Dr. Harris suggests that this attitude may develop if the baby is not loved, not wanted, and not properly cared for during the first two years. He suggests that if we live throughout our lives with this attitude we have a tendency to withdraw from society, from reality, and from others.

3. *I'm OK—You're not OK*. This third attitude is the attitude of criminals and other antisocial persons. This kind of person tries to manipulate people. Such persons go through life refusing to look inward.

4. *I'm OK—You're OK*. Dr. Harris suggests this fourth position is a mature attitude, an attitude for which we all should strive. The first three attitudes are grounded in emotions developed before we were two or three years old. He suggests that this more mature attitude can only be developed by thinking about what is important.

Perhaps this fourth attitude is not too far from the attitude that Jesus had in mind when he encouraged us to love our neighbor as ourselves. This does not mean that we overlook sin. Jesus accepted the adulterous woman as a person of worth although he deplored her sin (John 8:1-11). We must not allow old prejudices to undermine the faith we have in a new way to live. This new life of serving Jesus will make us happier and more productive. As adults we can choose not to respond as children but as mature people in Christ. Jesus loved his enemies. So can we.

The "Leap" and Some Big Problems

One of the speakers during the 1969 World Congress on Evangelism said that the three major problems in the world today are war, poverty, and racism. Each one of us might have a different list of problems and different suggestions as to what we should do about them. I encourage you to think of how one giant leap forward—a belief in the basic integrity and value of each person—relates to each of the following problems.

1. *Spiritual Alienation from God.* Some estimate that one-half of the world's population have never heard of Jesus Christ. We believe that Jesus is the Way, the Savior, the Truth. We believe that men are lost without him, that without God there is no hope. We believe that enlightenment is needed—that God is light, and in him is no darkness at all. Thus, if each person is of value, those who share these beliefs will work to make it possible for every person to hear about Jesus Christ and the way of salvation.

2. *Alienation from Each Other.* I believe that one of the big problems in the world today is the alienation of people from people. People do not love each other. They do not respect the personhood of each other. They do not know how to get along. If we believe in the value of each person, this is a giant leap forward in the area of interpersonal relationships. If we love our neighbor as ourselves, we will have fellowship with one another. If we see the value of a person as a person, we will treat everyone with kindness. I am not merely thinking about regard for people in the ghettos, or regard for people who are starving to death in India. I am also thinking about regard for people whom we encounter on a day-to-day basis. This is the test of what we really think about people.

3. *Poverty.* If my son were hungry, would I think that only his spiritual needs were important? Or, if I were hungry, would I go to church or to the grocery store? Are physical needs important? Is Christianity really person-centered? Do we love hungry people as we love ourselves?

4. *War.* Hate and greed are attitudes that are antagonistic to personhood, attitudes that lead to war. How to prevent wars in our imperfect world is a complicated problem. However, I am sure all of us would agree that there could be no war if all men took a giant leap forward and became person-centered.

5. *Loneliness.* Many people feel that they are alone even in a crowd. They feel that they know few people well. Instead, they know many people in a superficial way. Some children do not even know their own parents. One eighth–grade girl recently said, "I am one of eight children. My mother comes home from work, dead tired, and goes to bed. She doesn't have time for me. Neither does father. He don't like to talk to me. He don't know about my problems either. He told me the other night,

'Leave me alone. You just get me in trouble all the time. I am sick of you.'" This girl skips school, is very upset emotionally, and is expecting a child. She came to a school counselor to talk because she felt that her parents did not care.

A college girl with a high I.Q. was making straight F's after three quarters of work. She said: "My mother is always on my back. She tells me I am ugly, lazy, no good, and that I will never amount to anything. My father is dead. I feel that I am all alone although there are thousands of people around me. There must be an answer somewhere. There must be some meaning to life. If I could just drop out of school and enroll in a Vocational Training School, I think maybe everything would be all right."

Another college student said, "There must be happiness somewhere. I feel so alone. If I could just travel... I am afraid life will just pass me by, and I'll never be happy. Everybody seems to be picking at me. Life seems to be a matter of hard knocks leading to nowhere—like the man in *Easy Rider*, who finally gets killed along with most of his friends."

Conclusions

Perhaps we have never realized how much Christian fellowship can mean to people. Perhaps an improvement in our fellowship in the body of Christ would attract people to Christ and to the fellowship of warm, open, honest, concerned people. Certainly a belief in the integrity of the person would make us more sensitive to the feelings of those with whom we associate, would increase the quality of the fellowship in the body of Christ, and would make us more effective ambassadors for Christ.

The attitude expressed in the following lines can make a real difference in our lives:

> Grant that all may seek and find
> Thee a God supremely kind;
> Heal the sick, the captive free;
> Let us all rejoice in Thee,
> Let us all rejoice in Thee.

> —W. Hammond

O to be like Thee!
  Full of compassion,
Loving, forgiving, tender and kind,
  Helping the helpless,
Cheering the fainting,
  Seeking the wand'ring sinner to find.

O to be like Thee!
  O to be like Thee!
Blessed Redeemer, pure as Thou art;
  Come in Thy sweetness,
Come in Thy fullness;
  Stamp Thine own image
Deep on my heart.

—T. O. Chisholm

QUESTIONS FOR DISCUSSION

1. What do you think about the statement: "I'm O.K., You're O.K."?
2. If you feel that you are O.K., what evidence do you have that this is true?
3. If you feel that you are *not* O.K., what evidence do you have that *this* is true?
4. Are we always harder on ourselves than God is? What about the prodigal son and his father in this regard? Can you think of other relevant scriptures on this point?
5. What about scriptures in which God is harder on us than we are on ourselves?
6. What would you have to do differently to feel good about yourself?
7. Does God want us to feel good about ourselves?

7

How to Change Behavior

Most of us recognize the fact that behavior often needs changing. Some things need to be learned, others unlearned. We underlearn and overlearn. In the case of overlearning, we need to unlearn what we have learned; whereas, in the case of underlearning, we need to learn new behaviors. Phobias are examples of overlearning. Perhaps a person was whipped too severely by his parents and learned to be afraid of them and of others. This may mean that he withdraws from people and that he backs away in every conflict situation.

Schizophrenia may be related to underlearning. Some schizophrenics have never learned how to carry on normal conversations. Because of this fact, they may withdraw from people or attack them. They just do not know how to cope with people and so they react in various ways. They need to learn how to deal with people.

Learning New Behaviors

In stimulus-response terminology, deficit learning is accomplished through shaping. We reinforce the behavior that we wish to recur. We encourage people when they are doing what they should, and this will cause them to continue the behavior. Surplus learning means that there are bonds between stimuli and responses that should not be there. It is not rational for a person to be afraid of everyone he meets. In dealing with this problem, one of the best therapeutic approaches is to weaken or eliminate the bond that exists between the stimulus and the

61

response. This is sometimes done by means of catharsis or ex-
tinction. This is not as strong a method as that of systematic
desensitization in which relaxation is paired with the fear-
evoking stimuli to weaken or eliminate the strength of such
bonds. In either approach the behavior occurs but is not reinforced.

Spiritually we can change behavior in the same way. If we
have problems caused by underlearning, we need to learn
additional responses. Church leaders need to encourage healthy
spiritual behavior so that it will become fixed in a person's life.

One way of saying this is to say that we need to continue to
grow in Christ. We are inferior and need to continue to mature
and grow more like Christ. Peter tells us that "we should grow
in the grace and knowledge of our Lord and Savior Jesus Christ"
(II Peter 3:18). This means that we must accept the grace of God
and live according to his Word. It means that we should deal
honestly with both God and man. To be like Jesus we must be
forgiving, loving, zealous, obedient, and tenderhearted (Matt.
5:6; John 8; Luke 23; Eph. 4).

The Christian should learn to disagree without being disagreeable. To most people this means compromise, and since
compromise is not acceptable to them they shy away from even
admitting that a problem exists in this area. People outside the
church wonder why we are so disagreeable and cannot discuss
opposing viewpoints without becoming emotionally upset.
They do not understand the personal attacks some of us make
on our opponents. The apostle Paul learned to be all things to all
men that he might gain some for Christ (I Cor. 9:20–23). To the
Jews he became a Jew that he might gain the Jews. To the Gentiles he became a Gentile that he might gain them. To the weak
he became weak that he might gain the weak. In summary he
says, "And I do all things for the gospel's sake, that I may be a
joint partaker thereof" (I Cor. 9:23). If we could learn to disagree
with people intellectually without coming apart, withdrawing,
or attacking them in a cruel way, we could win more friends and
also win more people to Christ.

In order to function well as Christians, we need to learn certain ministerial skills. Paul writes of the various ministers in the
church. He mentions apostles, prophets, evangelists, pastors,
and teachers. These ministers were to support each member of
the body of Christ in the faith and knowledge of the Son of God
(Eph. 4:11–16).

We need to learn how to speak the truth in love and to grow in Christ. The body is framed and knit together through him. The body builds itself up in love by the strength that comes through Christ. We need to learn how to teach others. In fact, some in the early church should have been teachers, but they were still babes in Christ (Heb. 5:12–14). We need to learn how to do personal evangelism. We are taught that we might teach others. Paul taught Timothy and then said to him, "And the things which thou hast heard from me among many witnesses, the same commit thou to faithful men, who shall be able to teach others also" (II Tim. 2:2).

We need to learn how to visit the sick. James speaks of visiting the fatherless and the widows in their affliction (James 1:27). Others need visiting also. Visiting means more than just going and talking to someone. It means helping those who are in need. Perhaps they are in the emergency room of a hospital and need us to check on their house to see if the doors were left open, or sit with the children, or prepare the evening meal, or hem a new pair of pants for a child at home. Sometimes they need money. At other times a sensitive, listening ear may be the only need. All people in a hospital do not need the same thing. Much depends on whether the patient is in the emergency room, in intensive care, recovering from an operation, or just convalescing. Need depends on the situation. We need to be so sensitive that we recognize a need and so caring that we meet the need.

There are many other ministerial skills that are needed by all Christians. Many of us do not minister as Christians because we have never learned how. Church leaders need to sponsor programs to teach these skills.

We also need to learn how to cooperate with each other. The church cannot grow if no one cooperates. In fact, when no one cooperates the church is sick in much the same way as is a family in which a characteristic behavior is noncooperation. One person makes a statement and no one agrees or disagrees. The statement is just left hanging in the air. No alliances are formed and no real communication exists. Sometimes the church is like that. The elders try to lead, but no one is following. They try to teach, but no one listens.

In Romans 12:3–8 the church is said to be the body of Christ. Because members are parts of the body of Christ, we ought to respect others as well as ourselves. All members do not have the same office or function; but we all have work to do, and the work can be done best if we cooperate with each other. We cannot use the gifts that God by his grace has given us without cooperation. "Having gifts differing according to the grace that was given us, whether prophecy, let us prophesy according to the proportion of our faith; or ministry, let us give ourselves to our ministries; or he that teacheth, to his teaching; or he that exhorteth to his exhorting; he that giveth, let him do it with liberality; he that ruleth, with diligence; he that showeth mercy, with cheerfulness."

Another skill we need is how to overcome evil with good (Rom. 12:21). It is very difficult to just be good without doing good. Matthew recorded the story about an unclean spirit that had gone out of a man and passed through waterless places, seeking rest but not finding it. The evil spirit then went back to the man's house. It had been swept and garnished, but was still empty. He took with him seven other spirits more evil than himself. They entered the house and lived in it. This unusual story teaches us that it is hard for goodness to exist in a vacuum. We overcome evil by doing good.

A good illustration of this principle is seen in Ephesians 4:25–32. In that section of Scripture, there is an example of how we attack behaviors with other behaviors. We overcome falsehood by seeking truth, we overcome anger by settling our disputes before sundown, we overcome stealing by working in order to give, we overcome corrupt speech by edifying others, and we overcome bitterness and anger by being kind and forgiving. In each instance, the behavior to be learned is directly related to the problem and thus helps the person to overcome it. One behavior is substituted for another behavior. Thus, the old behavior is unlearned and the new behavior substituted. The connecting chain between the former stimulus and the response is weakened or eliminated, and the connecting chain between the new stimulus and response is strengthened. Thus, we become less like the devil and more like Christ.

Unlearning Old Behaviors

On the other hand, if the problem is *overlearning*, we need to unlearn some behaviors. The chains that connect stimuli and responses need to be weakened or eliminated. Many behaviors occur because of overlearning. Phobias are illustrations of this category. Phobic people are afraid of many things such as heights, people, animals, and closed in places. Such fears are exaggerated and irrational.

We are sometimes afraid of being nice to each other. Paul tells us in Romans 12:10 that we should be "tenderly affectioned one to another, . . . in honor preferring one another." It is wrong not to give honor where honor is due. It is healthy to be able to compliment another. It helps the giver and it reinforces good behavior in the receiver.

Sometimes good people are too afraid of God. Such fears may have been learned from parents who were too strict and punitive, or they may have been learned in other ways; but the fact remains, they have been learned. Such fears are difficult to unlearn.

A young man named Joe had often been whipped by his father until blood ran down his back. Joe did not believe that God could possibly accept him and love him. He felt very insecure and scared of God. In fact, when he thought of God he would break into tears and have a choking sensation. He had been conditioned to have too much fear of God.

The Bible helps us in such matters. We are told that perfect love casts out fear, and that there is no fear in love (I John 4:18). Very few Christians really believe this verse. They may think they believe it, but unconsciously they still fear God. Jesus is not a high priest who cannot be touched with a feeling of our infirmities "but one that hath been in all points tempted like as we are, yet without sin" (Heb. 4:15). Because he is this kind of divine being, we should "draw near with boldness to the throne of grace that we may receive mercy and may find grace to help us in time of need."

Many of us have also overlearned certain skills of criticism. We are good at picking at each other. Outsiders do not understand how we can say that we are following Jesus and be so critical of each other. We know how to dot the i's and cross the t's, but sometimes we overlook such things as love, mercy, and justice, the weightier matters of the law. Some well-recognized Christians have made a living by being professional critics. They seldom do anything of a constructive nature but are good at destroying someone else's work. Jesus himself has cautioned us to "judge not, that ye be not judged" (Matt. 7:1).

We must be careful not to judge the motives of others. An overly critical person beholds the mote in his brother's eye but does not consider the beam in his own. It is very difficult for him to admit that he has a problem. Jesus said to such a person, "Thou hypocrite, cast out first the beam out of thine own eye; and then shalt thou see clearly to cast out the mote out of thy brother's eye" (Matt. 7:5).

Doctrinal errors should be unlearned. The process for this begins with an attitude of seeking nothing but the truth. The next step is to go to the Bible and to read it to see what it actually teaches. The Bereans were more noble than were the people of Thessalonica in that "they received the word with all readiness of mind, examining the scriptures daily, whether these things were so" (Acts 17:11). We will never be able to see our own doctrinal errors until we read the Bible with an attitude that God is speaking to us through his Word. We need to ask what God's message is for us. The next step is to think in terms of how we can apply the teaching in order to improve our own behavior. If we just study from the point of trying to prove what we already believe, an unlearning of doctrinal errors is impossible. We will never allow God to correct our errors because we are constantly thinking in terms of correcting the errors of others.

A good example of this is racial prejudice. The person who is extremely prejudiced against someone of another race has great difficulty in seeing the intended message in Acts 10. God said to Peter that all men were clean in his sight. In Luke 10 Jesus commended the good Samaritan because he had done what was right. The Samaritan was the outcast, the usual object of prejudice. It is very difficult for the person who has been conditioned to be prejudiced to see what is meant by the Golden Rule (Matt. 7:12). We dismiss that message from our minds, and it does not weaken the chain between stimulus and response, between the thought of a person of another race and the response of prejudice. One way we dismiss God's message is by thinking of some behavior in the other person that seems to justify our prejudice against him or her. We may say that we are not prejudiced, that what we think is the truth. It is hard to understand how we can feel like this since Jesus was a person who accepted everyone as a person of value, made in the image of God. He was criticized for eating with publicans and sinners. Today we read this and still feel prejudice against the person who is down and out, or against the person of a minority race. The message of Christ does not sink into our hearts.

We need to do away with bad habits such as filthy language, using people for our advantage, bad health habits, thinking negative thoughts continually, feeling sorry for ourselves, being aggressive, or withdrawing from people. Paul tells us in Colossians 3:5–6: "Put to death therefore your members which are upon the earth: fornication, uncleanness, passion, evil desire, and covetousness, which is idolatry; for which things' sake cometh the wrath of God upon the sons of disobedience."

Thus, in order to grow spiritually, psychologically, or intellectually, we must attempt to unlearn. We must unlearn certain fears, certain criticism skills, certain doctrinal errors, as well as bad habits. Before we can be the kind of people we ought to be, we need to change these behaviors. We need to weaken these surplus responses and do away with them.

On the other hand, there are behaviors that we have not learned adequately. These behaviors need to be learned. Just as we need to learn good manners, we need to learn certain Christian characteristics in order to behave in a way that pleases Christ.

Conclusions

There are basically two approaches to changing behavior: unlearning inappropriate and immature behavior, and learning appropriate new responses. These two approaches should be used throughout our lives because we never get to a point where we do not need to unlearn and to learn. We always need to do away with behavior that causes us to be unhealthy and inadequate and to learn behavior that will be a positive influence in our lives, leading us to greater wholesomeness, health, maturity, and spirituality. God wants us to be healthy and effective.

Cutting loose from evil and coming to God are steps toward spiritual maturity, behavior changes that lead to joy and happiness. This weakens the influence of evil by meeting it directly with a response toward God. When we genuinely engage in such behavior we will be blessed. A lifestyle that has Christ at the center is a productive one. He is the Way, the Truth, and the

Life (John 14:6). He says to you, "Come unto me all ye that labor and are heavy laden, and I will give you rest" (Matt. 11:28). I hope you will accept the invitation to become a Christian (John 3:16; Luke 13:3; Rom. 10:10; Acts 2:38) and live a life of faithful service in fellowship with him and with his people (Rev. 2:10). Such a life is not lived in vain (Matt. 25; I Cor. 15:58).

QUESTIONS FOR DISCUSSION

1. Why does our behavior need changing?
2. Does behavior cause thinking or does thinking cause behavior?
3. What kind of thinking mistakes do you make?
4. What kind of action mistakes do you make?
5. How do thinking and actions affect feelings?
6. How do *you* change behavior?
7. Read Ephesians 4:17-32 and discuss Paul's method of changing behavior. What specific behaviors does he say should be changed?

Sex and the Bible

Sex and the Bible is a subject that needs studying for obvious reasons. We should apply God's Word to every sphere of our existence. If we do not apply his message on sex, we miss his guidance and direction in that area of our lives.

It is obvious that sex and its proper expression is a problem in our world today. It is the central theme of many television programs, books, films, comedies, and advertisements. "If it feels right, do it" is a current way of expressing this attitude of promiscuity. This hedonistic philosophy is a guide for many lives. The lust of the flesh overcomes the pull of God's Spirit (Gal. 5:19-24), as evidenced in homosexuality, fornication, and adultery. These practices are serious departures from God's way of righteousness.

Although homosexual acts are sinful (Rom. 1:18-32), we should have a great deal of patience with Christians who have tendencies toward homosexuality. It often takes a lot of patience, encouragement, time, and work, even with professional help, to overcome such problems. Overcoming is possible, though, through effort, reconditioning, and the help of true friends. Such help is inadequate without God, who sees the value of every person no matter what he or she has done.

The Causes of Sexual Problems

Conditioning in childhood is the strongest determinant of sexual sins. Children who do not know the Bible cannot be guided by its principles. Unrestrained nature is synonymous with pro-

miscuity. The best current research on the causes of homosexuality indicates that early conditioning is responsible, with a
few exceptions that may be caused by physiology. Children can be
taught homosexuality. A mother who treats a son as though he
is a daughter may cause that son to grow up to be homosexual.
He identifies more closely with his mother than with his father.
He thinks of himself as being female. Thus, when he begins to
date, he dates a male. On the other hand, a man who treats his
daughter as though she were his little boy may cause the same
problem in reverse. We ought to always treat our boys as boys
and our girls as girls. It is very helpful if the girl can be treated
from birth like a girl and can closely identify with her mother
during puberty and adolescence. The mother then becomes a
model for her and thus helps her develop a healthy self-concept.
Such girls think of themselves as being feminine and date boys.
Boys need to identify closely with their fathers. If they don't
have a father present in the home, they can sometimes identify
with another man, such as an uncle or a Sunday School teacher.

Whatever the causes of sexual problems, we need to talk
about them. It seems to me that we have gone through stages on
facing such matters honestly. First, no one wanted to talk about
it at all. I know one man who gets angry if his minister even says
the word *sex* in his sermons. Perhaps he never noticed that the
Bible contains many instructions on sex and its proper use. We
must not, therefore, avoid the subject because of our prior conditioning.

Next we went through a stage of saying that whatever is
wrong with a person sexually is a sickness: homosexual acts and
promiscuity are sicknesses. This may be so, but they are also
sins (Rom. 1:18–32). Now we need to begin a stage of working
through such problems to healthy solutions. This can be accomplished through determination, self-control, encouragement,
and relearning.

The Cure for Sexual Problems

In Genesis 1:27 and 28, we read that God created *male* and
female. Two sexes. He then told them to be fruitful and to multiply. Such instructions demand sex. In Genesis 1:31, after he had
created sexual beings and told them to be fruitful and to multi-

ply, he looked at everything that he had made and said that it was good. Then when he looked at the man and woman whom he had created male and female, he said that they were very good. Sex wasn't dirty; it was good. Adam and Eve were naked and were not ashamed. In Genesis 2:24 and 25, man was told to leave his father and mother and cleave to his wife, and they would become one flesh. A physical unity was to take place between a husband and his wife. Paul repeats this in the New Testament in Ephesians 5:23–31: Two become one flesh. God created sex and approves of it when it is not abused. Sex in itself is not dirty.

The Bible contains positive instructions on sex. To be fruitful and multiply is a positive endeavor. In Proverbs 5, the inspired writer first warns against the "strange woman." Her lips drop honey, and her mouth is smoother than oil. But her ways are unstable and in the end her feet go down to death. She is "as bitter as wormwood." The son is to stay away from such a woman, lest he lose his honor and perhaps his health as well.

But Solomon does not stop with these negative guidelines. In Proverbs 5:15, he begins giving positive instructions on sex. The son is to drink water out of his own cistern. His springs are not to be dispersed abroad. He is to rejoice in the wife of his youth: "Let her breasts satisfy thee at all times; and be thou ravished always with her love" (Prov. 5:19). Ecstasy between a husband and his wife is ordained by God. Heterosexuality in marriage is the teaching of God's Word. God made them male and female and told them to be fruitful and to multiply. He told them to enjoy their relationship physically as well as spiritually and emotionally. There should be ecstasy, communion, intimacy, and oneness in marriage. If we leave out physical excitation in a marriage because we believe sex is dirty, we have weakened God's plan for our home and shortchanged ourselves.

The Song of Solomon is a love story about a man and his wife. It exalts the husband–wife relationship. It teaches us that marriage should bring physical joy and spiritual happiness.

The New Testament has many passages on sex. In I Corinthians 7:1–5, Paul writes that a man should have a wife and a woman should have a husband. Both men and women have sexual needs that should be met by a partner in the marital relationship. Sexuality does not negate spirituality. God created sex. So one cannot correctly state that if a person is spiritual he will not be interested in sex. God himself endorsed the physical relationship in marriage.

In I Thessalonians 4:1–4, Paul writes that marriage involves more than sex. Marriage encompasses a total relationship, which includes holiness of character, purity, and honor. All of these things are vital in the marital relationship. Therefore, when a man is seeking a wife, he should consider more than just how she looks. When a woman wants to marry, she should be interested in more than just a handsome physique.

In Hebrews 13:4, the writer states that marriage is to be held in honor and that the marriage bed is to be undefiled. Some people thought that marriage was a lower level of existence, a lower level of spirituality, than was celibacy; sex was worldly and debased. This is untrue, although some people are still influenced by this point of view. Sex in marriage is good; sexual intercourse outside of marriage is forbidden.

In Ephesians 5:3–5, fornication is condemned; we are to flee youthful lusts according to II Timothy 2:22. This is in agreement with the commandment which says; "Thou shalt not commit adultery" (Exod. 20:14). In Matthew 19, Jesus recognized the validity of this teaching. In verse nine, he said, "Whosoever shall put away his wife, except for fornication, and shall marry another, committeth adultery: and he that marrieth her when she is put away committeth adultery." In a parallel passage, Jesus said, "Whosoever shall put away his wife, and marry another, committeth adultery against her: and if she herself shall put away her husband, and marry another, she committeth adultery" (Mark 10:11–12). Paul expressed the same general principle in Romans 7:2–3: "For the woman that hath a husband is bound by law to the husband while he liveth; but if the husband die, she is discharged from the law of the husband. So then if, while the husband liveth, she be joined to another man, she shall be called an adulteress: but if the husband die, she is free from the law, so that she is no adulteress: though she be joined to another man."

Jesus himself was present at a wedding feast in Cana of Galilee and thus endorsed marriage by his very presence at that particular wedding feast (John 2). Later in the first century, Paul said that those who were to fall away from the truth would forbid marriage (II Tim. 4:1–4). Our Lord's return will be like the husband and wife relationship in marriage (Rev. 19:7–9).

Heaven itself is like a marriage feast. Throughout the Bible marriage and sex in marriage are exalted. They are a part of God's plan for us.

Conclusions

Certain conclusions may be deduced from biblical teachings on sex. First, sex in itself is not dirty or debased. We damage our children when we imply that it is. We should be able to make a distinction between necessary sexual restraint and inhibiting all sexuality, a practice that hinders proper sexual expression after marriage. Second, heterosexuality is endorsed for marriage. Sex is to be between a man and a woman and not between a woman and a woman or between a man and a man (Rom. 1:18–32). Sex outside marriage is condemned in the Scriptures (Matt. 19:1–9; Mark 10:1–11; Rom. 7:1–4; I Cor. 6:9–11; Matt. 5:31–32). Fornication is a work of the flesh (Gal. 5:19–21). No fornicator "hath any inheritance in the kingdom of Christ and God" (Eph. 5:3–5) but will have his part "in the lake that burneth with fire and brimstone" (Rev. 21:8). Living together as husband and wife outside of marriage is wrong. Some church members think that the Bible says nothing about such activities.

We must give our children a balanced approach to human sexuality. God's purpose is clear. When he created male and female, he approved heterosexuality. When he says to be fruitful and to multiply, he requires heterosexuality. A man and a woman multiply. Homosexuals cannot multiply! Nature as God created it implies heterosexuality, as evidenced by the nature of sex organs and the population balance between the sexes: there are approximately 50 percent men and 50 percent women in all countries of the world. It is this way because God created them male and female, and he wanted them to be fruitful and to multiply.

Certain people have a scriptural right to marry: (1) those who have never been married before, (2) those whose mates have died (Matt. 19:5), and (3) innocent parties whose mates have committed fornication (Matt. 19:9). All others who have married have no clear-cut biblical assurance that they have a right to continue in such marriages.

The Bible is against homosexual acts. In Genesis 19 we read an unusual story about Lot in Sodom. When angels came to visit him, the men of the city wanted *to know* them. Lot refused: "Do not bother these two men," he said. "I don't want you *to know* these two men. You can have my two daughters and do with them whatever you want to do, if you leave these men alone sexually." This strong position was taken against homosexual acts and against abuse of guests. "To know" these men was to have sexual acts with them. This same usage is found in Matthew 1:24–25. Mary was with child and Joseph "knew her not" until after the child was born. God was so upset with Sodom's sins that he condemned the city and told Lot to flee from the city to avoid its impending destruction. He then condemned Sodom and Gomorrah and burned them to the ground. Our word *sodomy* is derived from the homosexual acts committed in the city of Sodom.

The New Testament clearly condemns homosexual acts. Romans 1:26–28 deals specifically with acts against nature: "For this cause God gave them up unto vile passions; for their women changed the natural use into that which is against nature: and likewise also the men, leaving the natural use of the woman, burned in their lust one toward another, men with men working unseemliness, and receiving in themselves that recompense of their error which was due. And even as they refused to have God in their knowledge, God gave them up unto a reprobate mind, to do these things which are not fitting."

Another relevant passage is I Corinthians 6:9–11. The word *effeminate* is translated in the Revised Standard Version as "homosexuals," or "sexual perverts" (v. 9). The unrighteous, idolaters, adulterers, fornicators, thieves, drunkards, revilers, extortioners, and homosexuals shall not inherit the kingdom of God. This does not mean that God will not save them if they turn to him. God is not going to save them in that condition. It is not a matter of being able to choose one's sexual lifestyle. It is a matter of God's plan. Some of them had been homosexuals (I Cor. 6:11), but they "were washed, sanctified, and justified in the name of the Lord Jesus Christ, and in the Spirit of God."

Jude 7 and 8 make the same point: "Even as Sodom and Gomorrah, and the cities about them, having in like manner with these given themselves over to fornication and gone after strange flesh, are set forth as an example, suffering the punishment of eternal fire. Yet in like manner these also in their dreamings defile the flesh, and set at nought dominion, and rail at dignities." In modern translations "strange flesh" is translated "homosexual acts." Jude's point is that the people he was condemning would be punished as were homosexuals in Lot's day.

God ordains heterosexuality. He wants a husband and a wife to be infatuated sexually with each other and to become one in flesh as well as spirit. He wants love to be an integral part of sex so that sex will not be impersonal but a tool of love and communication. People are not to be used and abused as things but respected and helped as sensitive people in accordance with God's eternal plan. Such an approach will help us to work through our problems and to be happy and enriched as children of God.

If there are sexual problems, then we can handle those just as we do other problems. We analyze the problem and try to solve it. Relearning requires persistence and patience. We must not be molded by the world but rather be molders of it (Rom. 12:1–2; Matt. 5:13–16). Having a sexual fling will not relieve pent-up sexual feelings. God's way is to influence our minds and to direct us into a lifestyle dedicated to clean living. We should develop wholesome attitudes toward all people. This includes homosexuals. We should not mistreat them. They should be encouraged to control their homosexual inclinations and get therapy to help them feel normal sexually. God's Word leads us to a better way.

If you have been sinned against by your prior conditioning, by your training, to be homosexual, remember: (1) that God loves you still, and (2) that whatever can be learned can be unlearned and whatever can be conditioned can be unconditioned. It is also helpful to remember that your cross is not unlike the cross of many others in this regard. Both you and they must refrain from doing what is wrong. The Christian heterosexual man may want to sleep with a beautiful woman who is not his wife, but he does not. The Christian man with homosexual tendencies may want to commit sexual acts with another man, but he does not. "Satan may call, the world may entreat me, but there is no voice that answers within." Paul's admonition to "be angry and sin not" (Eph. 4:26) is a similar application of this principle of Christian restraint. We cannot always do what we feel like doing.

In Romans 7:18–25, Paul said that he could not always do that which he willed to do because evil was present in his flesh, and he saw "a different law in my members, warring against the law of my mind, and bringing me into captivity under the law of sin which is in my members." What was his answer? Christ. Jesus delivered him from his body of sin and death. This may sound too simple for you, but Christ can be your answer too. His spirit can empower you, his blood can cleanse you of your sins. He does not call for perfection but for faithfulness. You will continue to have evil thoughts, but you can control your actions. You can "be angry and sin not."

QUESTIONS FOR DISCUSSION

1. Is it wrong to talk about sex?
2. What is fornication?
3. What is adultery?
4. Is it possible for a homosexual to go to heaven?
5. What implications are there in this chapter for sex education?
6. How far should a couple go before marriage?
7. How can couples settle differences of opinion about sex: frequency, romance, different desires, foreplay . . .?

Overcoming Grief

Grief is an inward reaction to the loss of something or someone we love. We may experience grief from many diverse causes. Grief may come when we fail to receive a coveted promotion, or when a child's behavior disappoints us. It may plague us when a beloved son or daughter marries and leaves home. Reverses in health or sudden physical impairment often trigger grief. But most commonly, and perhaps in its deepest form, grief comes when we suffer the loss by death of someone near and dear to us. Any and all of these losses cause human beings to suffer. Jesus wept when he saw the deep grief of Mary and Martha as they mourned the death of their brother Lazarus.

Since grief cannot be avoided by any of us, we are faced with the problem of how best to bear up under it and work our way through it with the least emotional trauma. Experience has shown that some of us are more adept at overcoming grief than others. Can we learn ways that will help us work through loss, disappointment, and grief?

Ten Steps to Overcoming Grief

1. *Learn certain facts about grief.* There are at least three stages of grief: shock, suffering, and recovery. During the stage of shock, actions are mechanical. One feels numb, dazed, depressed, guilty, angry, sorry for oneself, frustrated, disinterested, and alone. One may withdraw from people, become aggressive, cry profusely, clam up, bottle up grief, do strange things, deny the

death, distort the truth by claiming perfection for the one who has died. Restlessness, loss of sleep, and failure to eat properly are other reactions during the stage of shock, which usually lasts from a few moments to a few days. Should it last longer than this the grief may become pathological, and professional counseling may be necessary.

The second stage is that of suffering. Denial of the death is no longer possible. It now becomes all too clear that a loved one is gone, irrevocably so, and that nothing will ever be the same again. The hurt is deep indeed. This stage may begin immediately after the death, during the funeral, or immediately after the funeral. It constitutes the worst suffering most of us have to bear. Friends have gone and one begins to feel the burden of being alone. One may feel so frustrated that rash and hasty decisions are made. Decisions on the disposition of property should be postponed until much later when one is able to cope rationally with such matters. Or the person may quit a job, move to another state, or get married because the pain of grief is so unbearable. On the other hand, the person may withdraw from others and have very little to do with anybody. This is a time of feeling frustrated over bank accounts, wills, insurance, and other problems. It is a time of learning to deal with people who do not understand how deeply you are hurt and who feel that you should put the death behind you and go on as if it had never happened.

The third stage, recovery, should come before too many weeks or months. However, a year or two is often needed to really get back to normal again. During this stage actions become normal again. One learns to deal with ideas as well as with emotions, to live in the present and to look forward to the future. He learns to communicate with others, to develop a normal social life, and to gradually regain his sense of identity. He no longer has to force his actions as he did during the stage of suffering; actions become free and normal. In this stage the person may renew his association with old friends and cultivate new ones. His personality is more outgoing, and he looks at himself realistically and perhaps sets new goals. He may be better disciplined and begin to adjust to the future with confidence. Just understanding these stages may help a person to successfully work through his grief.

A specific phenomenon that is common to those who are

working through grief is that of strange experiences and actions that seem unnatural and threatening. The person may suspect that he is losing control of himself or going crazy. One widow reported such feelings several days after her husband's funeral. She came home from shopping and mechanically went through the motions of putting up groceries. Suddenly she was aware that she had put a roll of bathroom tissue in the refrigerator. For weeks after the funeral her behavior reflected this absent-minded approach.

Many others have related the experience of "seeing their departed mate." The experience seems real to them. One widow had a dream about her husband, who had died several months before. Her dream tied in closely with a particular habit that her husband had of smoking in bed. She had been fearful of his catching the house on fire. In her dream she smelled smoke. In fact, when she awakened she smelled the scent of smoke in the room and believed that he had returned and was actually in the room with her. She was deeply offended when friends suggested that she was imagining the smell of smoke. She insisted that she did smell smoke. I believe that the smell of smoke was stored in her memory. This memory was stirred when she dreamed of her husband. Understanding that such experiences can occur and are considered normal may help a person to overcome grief.

This brings us to another topic, that of the difference between normal and abnormal grief. All of the stages that we have discussed previously—shock, suffering, and recovery—are stages of grief that most people experience. If these stages are prolonged, a need for professional help may be indicated. So might other prolonged reactions such as somatic distress, preoccupation with the image of the deceased, abnormal guilt feelings, extreme hostile reactions, and a radical change in patterns of conduct. Such a person may become completely disinterested in life, both in the present and future. He may be completely absorbed and obsessed by the person who has died. Such a person should be encouraged to get professional counseling. Even with abnormal grief, it is possible to return to a normal way of life, a life that may be different but still meaningful and profitable.

2. *Admit the loss.* Denial of death or an impending divorce will hinder recovery by prolonging the grief. A person who is contemplating divorce stays in a state of turmoil until the divorce is

final. Recovery is impossible until the divorce is final. One cannot admit a loss while there is still hope. Adjustment is also difficult with divorced persons because there is often conflict over the divorce. Old feelings and sores are agitated by continued contact during the divorce settlement and even after the divorce. Grief may be more severe for a divorced person than for one whose mate has died. Another reason that grief may be more difficult for divorced persons is that society does not recognize the severity of such grief and does not aid in working through it. The grief is complicated by the stigma that is attached to one who is divorced. The divorced person may feel rejected and discouraged and think that everyone assumes that he is at fault and is a failure.

One man who had lost his wife said, "There are still some more pages in my life's book that I plan to write." He had successfully worked through his grief because he had been willing to admit the loss and to put it in the past. On the other hand, one widow decided that she did not want to prolong her grief even by going to the funeral. She went instead on a fun-filled vacation to Florida. As a result she experienced a nervous breakdown six months later. She had not permitted herself the necessary grief and recovery processes because she was denying that death had occurred.

3. *Talk it out.* Old memories are not going to be forgotten and should not be forgotten. They need to be talked out so that when they recur they will be familiar memories with which you have learned to live. It is useless and often depriving to try to avoid memories. They will continue to come. They may, if you work through them promptly, come less frequently and with less adverse effects, but they will continue to come. They can enrich your life for as long as you live if you will learn to live with them and put them in proper perspective.

Sometimes a grieving person is angry at the one who left him, be it daughter, mother, wife, or husband. One may feel abandoned and may wonder why the other person left him in such a situation. Sometimes the grieving person is angry at the doctor and accuses him of not doing everything he could have done. Sometimes the minister is the object of anger: "He did not visit us as he should have. He said the wrong thing at the funeral." At times the anger may be turned inward and lead to depression. Therefore, it is imperative that anger be brought out and discussed with a friend, a minister, or someone who will listen sympathetically. Such anger may then be worked through and hostility toward others avoided. Both hostility and anger are common reactions to grief and should be faced, discussed, and resolved.

It is also important to talk about guilt feelings. Some of these may be the result of true guilt. In such a case, you should do what is necessary to relieve such guilt: turn to God, obey his Word, and accept his forgiveness.

The guilt people experience at the death of a loved one is usually false guilt. The person should not feel guilty. He has done everything that reasonable and prudent people would expect of him, but he still blames himself. For example, one widow said that if she had not allowed her husband to go to the grocery store that he would not have died, since he had a heart attack in a grocery store and died there. He had a history of heart trouble so there is no reason to believe the heart attack was caused by his going to the grocery store. He probably would have had it even if he had stayed at home. This woman continued to torture herself with such accusations for several years after her husband's death.

Another type of false guilt feelings is more difficult to solve. In such cases, the person may feel that if he had taken his mate to the doctor earlier the death would not have occurred. This could be true, but there was no way to know this until it was too late. It is a matter of feeling guilty for not having the ability to know the future.

A special case in point is that of suicide. The relatives of one who has committed suicide will often blame themselves. They will say that if they had been the kind of people they should have been, had taken the person to see a professional counselor, had been nicer to the person, that their relative would not have committed suicide. This seldom is factual, but one fact is sure: since we are not God, there is no way that we can know what is going on inside the mind of another human being.

Sometimes couples who are extremely close are broken up because of the tragic suicide of one of them. The other is completely surprised, hurt, and frustrated. There may be a medical problem that is unknown. There may be a chemical imbalance in the brain of such a person that is inherited or caused by some physiological factor that is unknown. At any rate, the solution is never simple, and relatives should not blame themselves for not being perfect. With God's help, they can adjust and live a meaningful life.

Guilt feelings need to be discussed and brought out in the open. One widow who felt guilty about her husband's death finally discussed these feelings in one of our groups. Her medical doctor was not surprised that her "nervous rash" disappeared within a day or two after she engaged in group discussion. There is tremendous value in talking about memories of the departed loved one, about anger and guilt feelings.

4. *Express your grief.* When the death of a loved one occurs, a person feels shocked, hurt, frustrated, disappointed, and sometimes angry. He may feel hemmed in and so disturbed that he feels as though he is going to burst. He wants to express his feelings but often does not. In our society we are discouraged from crying. We tell our sons especially that they should not cry. Even when they are little boys, we tell them that little boys don't cry.

God created tear ducts; they must have a purpose. If they cannot be used to express our sorrow, what are they for? Jesus himself wept (John 11:35). He had lost a friend. Lazarus, brother of Mary and Martha, had died. They were grieving because of his death. Christians are told to weep with those who weep (Rom. 12:15). When King David's child was sick, he prayed to God for the child, fasted, and wept (II Sam. 12:15–23). David was a man of strength. The Bible never calls grieving weakness. It is not grieving but the way of grieving that matters. In I Thessalonians 4:13, Paul writes: "Grieve not as those who have no hope." There is hope if we trust in God. He gives meaning to death and to life.

If one fails to grieve and bottles up his feelings, he is storing up a great deal of difficulty that may affect his life adversely later on. One woman, for example, promised her husband that she would never cry because of his death. She kept that promise but had ulcers within six months after the funeral. During one of our group sessions, she broke down and told about the long struggle during the time her husband suffered with cancer. After she had cried and talked this out, she began to recover. Later she obtained a job in a funeral home and was able to help many other grieving widows.

5. *Force yourself back into circulation.* During grief one may not

feel like seeing anyone or doing anything. One may prefer staying at home to going to work, church, or other social gatherings. One just does not feel like talking with anybody. However, to continue such withdrawal from normal activities will reinforce negative feelings and will aggravate problems. There is a time, especially during the suffering stage, when one will need to force oneself to do certain things: meet new people, cultivate old friends, resume normal religious activities, go back to work, begin a hobby, and interact with people. Such activities will prepare one to resume a normal lifestyle.

One will also need to perform certain activities that may be unfamiliar and that one has never done before. A man whose wife has died may need to do housework, take care of clothing, supervise the children, and do other things he may seldom have done while his wife was alive. A woman whose husband has died may be completely unfamiliar with a number of maintenance jobs around the house for which she must now be responsible. She may have to cope for the first time with bank accounts, wills, insurance, tax returns, and other matters. All of these things her husband may have done while he was with her. If she cannot do these things, she must force herself to seek help.

6. *Learn to adjust to a new identity.* When one loses someone who is very close, one's identity often changes. Whether the loss is that of a father, a child, a husband, or a wife, the way one thinks about oneself often changes at the death of a loved one. A widow has difficulty in describing her identity. Is she single? Married? If she dates, will she feel guilty because she still thinks of herself as a wife who must be loyal to her husband? She feels single but not in the same way that she did before she was married. She feels married but not in the same way that she did before her husband died. She is not accustomed to being called a widow. Does she remarry too soon because she cannot get used to her new identity? Sometimes this is a real problem.

For a widower there are similar questions. Is he a husband? Single? Will he feel guilty when he dates? Will he grow in his new role? A teenage boy may have similar identity adjustments when his father dies. Is he still a boy? Does the death of his father in itself suddenly make him a man? Parents sometimes force their sons to become men too soon.

Divorced persons may have identity problems. They do not feel

exactly single—not in the same way that they felt before they
were married. They do not feel married in the same sense that
they were before they were divorced. They do not enjoy being
called divorced. They feel that this places a stigma on them.
They sometimes feel that they are not allowed to be happy. They
may be single but do not feel that they have the right to remarry
again.

The adjustment to a new identity is very important to future
happiness. The loss of someone close to us necessitates grap-
pling with identity questions before adjustment and personal
growth are possible.

7. *Do something about your depression.* Depression and grief are
often related. People seldom work through grief without ex-
periencing periods of depression. They feel sad, gloomy, and
are inactive. They have a tendency to withdraw from others, but
the more they withdraw, the more depressed they become.
They may lose sleep, or they may wake up early in the morning.
They may not eat properly.

A depressed person can force himself into a normal lifestyle.
One way to do this is to write down some things that one likes to
do or once liked to do. I suggest making a list of perhaps fifteen
or twenty activities. The next step is to put them on one's calen-
dar for a week. Then begin to pursue these activities, checking
them off as they are done. If these are positive, reinforcing
events, one should begin to feel happier. This is one way of
attacking depression that is associated with inactivity. It may
change your lifestyle and your feelings.

When one is depressed, the example of Elijah (I Kings 19) is
good to remember. As you may recall, Elijah had been victorious: he had called upon God, and God had heard and accepted
his offering (I Kings 17–18). In contrast, Baal did not respond to
the continuous call of 450 of his prophets. After the death of the
prophets of Baal, Jezebel, the wife of King Ahab, threatened to
take the life of Elijah. Elijah reacted the way most of us would:
he was scared, disappointed, and disillusioned. His dreams
were shattered. His life was coming apart. He withdrew to a
juniper tree and later on to a cave. He seemed to have both a
sleeping and an ea'ing problem. He wanted to die.

God reminded Elijah of his continued concern. He told Elijah
that there were seven thousand knees that had not bowed to
Baal. He also told Elijah that he had something to live for: he

should go and appoint Hazael as king over Syria, Jehu as king over Israel, and Elisha as prophet in his place. Encouraged, Elijah followed God's plan and continued to live a profitable life. In a like manner, we can follow the example of Elijah.

8. *Serve others.* Often when we are grieving, our thoughts are turned inward. While it is sometimes good to look inward, continuous reflection on our feelings often leads to depression. At such times we need to look outward and upward. We need to think not only in terms of our own faults but also in terms of our good points as well. We need to think of serving others. Give a cup of cold water to someone in the name of the Lord. Jesus said that this is a valid test of what life really ought to be: service to others. Visit those who are in prison. Feed those who are hungry. Help those who are in need (Matt. 25:31–46).

I remember one widow who was having an especially difficult time with her grief. She was very close to her husband and felt very inadequate without him. She described her feelings as one who had lost part of herself when she lost her husband. She listened to our comments about looking outward, and the next week when she came to the group, she had a contagious smile on her face, a smile of joy. Everyone noticed it and asked her what had happened. She said, "Well, I've turned the corner. This last week I did something that I used to really enjoy doing: I baked some cookies. I then took them to an older widow who lives across the street from me, and it just changed my life. It made me feel completely different. At that point, my life really began to change. I think I'm on the right road now."

Service can make a difference if we will give our lives to the service of others and trust God. Such a life will not be lived in vain.

9. *Set your sail in the direction in which you wish to go in your life.* Did you ever study the stimulus-response principle of psychology? The idea is that you can analyze behavior from the point of view of stimulus and response. A certain stimulus occurs, and that causes a certain response. For example, I might ask you a question, and that stimulus might cause you to respond in a certain way. Or perhaps a better illustration would be that a doctor might tap your knee, and that stimulus would cause your foot to move.

A more meaningful paradigm, which followed the S-R principle, is the S-O-R approach to the study of behavior. Behavior is not just a matter of stimulus and response but a matter of the organism as well. The organism can influence the response. What a person thinks can influence the response. The same stimulus for two different people can cause two different responses. For example, two different teenagers may be offered a drink. One of them responds by drinking, whereas the other responds by refusing the offer. The organism influenced the response.

Here is a little poem that is very meaningful to me:

> One ship travels east,
> Another travels west,
> By the self-same wind that blows:
> Tis the set of the sail,
> And not the gale,
> That determines the way that it goes.

This poem's author is unknown to me, but its meaning is valuable. It may seem to be too simple an approach for complex problems; however, this need not be the case. Its main point is that you can influence the course of your life.

One way to analyze your behavior is to think in terms of what you say to yourself about yourself in various situations. This influences your behavior. The same stimulus can cause a ship to go either east or west, depending on the way the person sets the sail. The same stimulus can cause one behavior or its opposite behavior, depending on what a person is saying to himself. The same fire that melts the butter hardens the egg. The same discipline that makes a man out of one boy may destroy another. It depends on what is going on inside the boys at the time.

What I am encouraging you to do is to think about where you want to go with the remaining part of your life: remember, your life isn't over yet. Do you remember the movie in which Andy Griffith played a minister? A stranger drove by and stopped to talk to Andy: "Lived here all your life?" the stranger asked. "Not yet," replied Andy with his usual pleasant smile. He had some more living to do, and so do you. There will be plenty of time to stop living when the time comes at some future point. Live in the present and in the future, not in the past.

Analyze what you are saying to yourself. A grieving person may be saying to himself, "I'll never take the chance of losing anyone else I love. I'll just never love anyone else again. I'll never get close to anyone else. I'll keep to myself." This is one way of protecting oneself, but it is not the best way. One's life can be enriched by allowing others to get close and in sharing one's life with others. If no risk is taken, there is no chance for gain.

We can always be thankful for the memories we have of our loved ones. Those memories can never be taken away but will be with us always and enrich our lives. We can be thankful for that and know that if we had to place the life of our departed loved one on a debit–credit ledger there would be more on the credit side than on the debit side. Therefore, we have many things for which to be thankful. Our lives are certainly richer because of our having known and lived with our loved ones than they would have been had we never known them. If we can say such things to ourselves, the response may be quite different than it would be otherwise.

If you decide your life is over, it probably is. You can choose this route, and you may feel like doing so, but this is a tragic mistake. God has given you life for a purpose, and you need to use it in a good way. Enjoy what God has placed before you. Notice the aroma of food, the greenness in the grass, the beauty of flowers and trees, the smile of little children, the sunrise, and the sunset. If you broaden your interests so that your entire life is not focused on one thing, everything will have a better chance of falling into its proper place, and you will have a better chance of living a full and complete life.

10. *Lean on God.* There are three verses of Scripture that at first glance seem to be contradictory:

(1) Galatians 6:5: "For each man shall bear his own burden."
(2) Galatians 6:2: "Bear ye one another's burdens, and so fulfil the law of Christ."
(3) Psalm 55:22: "Cast thy burden upon Jehovah, and he will sustain thee: He will never suffer the righteous to be moved."

All three of these verses are meaningful. There are some problems that one must bear himself. There are other problems that others can help us bear. There are still other problems that one needs to cast upon the Lord.

A number of Bible passages are helpful at this point. They emphasize the fact that God cares and that faith in him can help us to find meaning in our lives. The 23rd Psalm is perhaps the most comforting passage in the Bible for those who are struggling through grief. People like to remember that the Lord is their Shepherd and that he will take care of their wants. It is especially meaningful to remember that it is possible to fear no evil because God is with us. He comforts us. What comfort it is to believe that "surely goodness and mercy shall follow me all the days of my life; and I shall dwell in the house of the Lord forever."

In Psalm 46 God is represented as a refuge and strength, a very present help in time of trouble. The psalmist concludes, "Therefore will we not fear, though the earth do change, and though the mountains be shaken into the heart of the seas; though the waters thereof roar and be troubled, though the mountains tremble with the swelling thereof." God is with us, and we should not be afraid. Verse 7 continues by stating, "The Lord of hosts is with us; the God of Jacob is our refuge."

In Psalm 121 the psalmist lifts up his eyes unto the hills because his help comes from the Lord who made heaven and earth. Verse 3 states, "He will not suffer thy foot to be moved; He that keepeth thee will not slumber." The Lord is thought of in this Psalm as man's keeper, his shade, his protection. The psalmist concludes in verses 7 and 8 with these words: "Jehovah will keep thee from all evil; He will keep thy soul. Jehovah will keep thy going out and thy coming in from this time forth and for evermore."

In the New Testament there are many comforting passages. John 14:1–3 is often helpful to grieving persons.

> Let not your heart be troubled: believe in God, believe also in me. In my Father's house are many mansions; if it were not so, I would have told you; for I go to prepare a place for you. And if I go and prepare a place for you, I come again, and will receive you unto myself; that where I am, there ye may be also.

These verses give hope to Christians. They look for Christ's return, when he will receive them unto himself, and they will live with him in complete happiness throughout eternity.

The emphasis in I Corinthians 15 is on a subject that is always thought of by grieving persons, the resurrection of the dead. Those who return to dust will be raised from the dead. Paul states that Christ's resurrection is proof of our resurrection.

"The last enemy that shall be abolished is death" (I Cor. 15:26). A bodily resurrection is assured. Paul says:

> So also is the resurrection of the dead. It is sown in corruption; it is raised in incorruption: it is sown in dishonor; it is raised in glory: it is sown in weakness; it is raised in power: it is sown a natural body; it is raised a spiritual body. If there is a natural body, there is also a spiritual body (I Cor. 15:42–44).

The thought is that the body is not now suited for eternity. It must be changed, and it will be changed in the resurrection of the dead. Flesh and blood cannot inherit the kingdom of God; neither can corruption inherit incorruption. We must be changed. This will happen at the last trumpet when the dead shall be raised.

Paul continues in I Corinthians 15:53–57 by stating:

> For this corruptible must put on incorruption, and this mortal must put on immortality. But when this corruptible shall have put on incorruption, and this mortal shall have put on immortality, then shall come to pass the saying that is written, Death is swallowed up in victory. O death, where is thy victory? O death, where is thy sting? The sting of death is sin; and the power of sin is the law: but thanks be to God, who giveth us the victory through our Lord Jesus Christ.

Because of the resurrection, we should be steadfast and unmoveable, always abounding in the work of the Lord because we know that our work is not in vain (I Cor. 15:58).

I'd like to briefly mention two relevant passages from the book of II Corinthians. In II Corinthians 4, beginning in verse 16, Paul discusses the inner person and the outer person. The outer person may be deteriorating, but the inner person is renewed day by day. The inner person is becoming more and more like Jesus at the same time that the outer person is losing ground. At the beginning of chapter 5, Paul continues, "For we know that if the earthly house of our tabernacle be dissolved, we have a building from God, a house not made with hands, eternal, in the heavens." While we are in this body, we are absent from the Lord. The real person is one's spirit, which in death returns to God. The real person is not buried in the cemetery but goes back to God (II Cor. 5:1–10). This kind of faith gives meaning to both life and death.

The second passage from II Corinthians is found in chapter 12. Here Paul gives some unusual revelations that came to him from his experiences in the third heaven. Because of these revelations, God gave him a thorn in the flesh. Paul pleaded with God three times for this thorn to be removed. God did not remove the thorn but told him, "My grace is sufficient for thee; for my power is made perfect in weakness." Paul concludes by writing, "Wherefore I take pleasure in weaknesses, in injuries, in necessities, in persecutions, in distresses, for Christ's sake; for when I am weak, then am I strong" (II Cor. 12:10).

Philippians 4:4-9, 13, and 19 are among my favorite passages of Scripture. They are written by a joyful prisoner who encourages us to rejoice in the Lord.

> In nothing be anxious; but in everything by prayers and supplication with thanksgiving let your requests be made known unto God. And the peace of God, which passeth all understanding, shall guard your hearts and your thoughts in Christ Jesus" (Phil. 4:6-7).

Paul tells us in verse 8 to think on things that are "honorable, just, pure, lovely, and of good report." Then after having thought on such things, we are encouraged to put these thoughts into action: "These things do: and the God of peace shall be with you" (Phil. 4:9). Notice the relationship between thinking, doing, and feeling. Peace follows pure thoughts and upright behavior. Verse 13 of this same chapter is especially meaningful to me. It expresses confidence in God in these words: "I can do all things in him that strengtheneth me."

Hebrews 13:5 states a principle that is repeated several times in the Bible. The principle is that God will never leave us or forsake us. He promised this to Moses and to Joshua. He repeats the promise to us. Jesus himself also made this promise when he said, "I am with you always, even unto the end of the world" (Matt. 28:20). God is present during our moments of grief. The same power that raised Jesus from the dead is at work in us (Eph. 1:19).

Another meaningful passage is I John 4:8, which states that "God is love." This is especially meaningful during grief because during such times we sometimes forget that God still loves us. We tend to think that if he loved us he would not have allowed our loved ones to die or our mate to break up our marriage. Personally, I do not believe that God comes down and strikes people dead or that he actively breaks up marriages. Death may be thought of in terms of natural laws or in terms of God's passive will but not in terms of his active will. When someone dies in a car wreck, I do not believe that God took hold of the wheel and caused the car to wreck. We need to repeat to ourselves that "God is love." In him we can have hope, and we can have faith that he is still with us, that he cares when our hearts are grieved.

One final book of the Bible should be mentioned, the Book of Revelation. There are two passages that are especially meaningful to me in terms of grief. The first one, Revelation 14:13, states: "And I heard a voice from heaven saying, Write, Blessed are the dead who die in the Lord from henceforth: yea, saith the Spirit, that they may rest from their labors; for their works follow with them." Being in the Lord is the key to eternal rest. Our works are not forgotten; they follow us. Another translation says, "They follow after him." We can honor our relatives who have died by being influenced by their righteous lives.

The last passage I wish to mention is found in Revelation 21, a very beautiful section of Scripture describing the Christian's hope:

> And I saw a new heaven and a new earth: for the first heaven and the first earth are passed away; and the sea is no more. And I saw the holy city, new Jerusalem, coming down out of heaven from God, made ready as a bride adorned for her husband. And I heard a great voice out of the throne saying, Behold, the tabernacle of God is with men, and he shall dwell with them, and they shall be his people, and God himself shall be with them, and be their God: and he shall wipe away every tear from their eyes; and death shall be no more; neither shall there be mourning, nor crying, nor pain, any more: the first things are passed away.

Faith can give meaning to us in time of difficulty. This does not mean that we will not hurt, but it does mean that we can find satisfactory answers to our grief. Where answers stop short, trust in God can enable us to continue to live for him and to look to the future with faith that all things will work together for good because we love him (Rom. 8:28). Since God is for us, who can be against us (Rom. 8:31–39)?

The steps we have discussed can help us work through grief. We should remember that those for whom we grieve would not want us to stop living, and God does not want us to stop living. He wants our lives to be meaningful and happy, and he will help us to lead productive lives in his service. I hope you will find and accept God's answer for your life.

QUESTIONS FOR DISCUSSION

1. How would *you* describe grief?
2. What stages do people sometimes go through in grief?
3. Do people grieve over things other than the loss of a loved one by death? What sorts of other things?
4. What are some differences and similarities between grief over divorce and grief because of death?
5. What sorts of losses have you suffered? What was it like?
6. What are some scriptures that helped you?
7. How may we help others who grieve?

10

The Unhappy Home

There are many trials in the home because in the home we live on a close, intimate basis. One man, for example, wanted to be very righteous. First he went to the top of a mountain to meditate. Later, when this didn't seem to work, he came home and sat on top of the kitchen table to meditate day after day. When the family objected to this practice, he said, "It is very hard to be a saint in one's own home." The reason for this is that it is very hard to be righteous in a practical way. It is harder to be a Christian on a one-to-one basis than to say that we love people in the abstract—that we love someone in another country whom we have never met. But Christianity really is loving people on a one-to-one basis.

What are some typical mistakes made in the home? You can list many, but I want to mention briefly the following three mistakes: wrong goals, wrong behavior, and failure to live by certain positive principles outlined in the Word of God. All of these mistakes ultimately lead to unhappiness.

Goals

Goals have a great deal to do with behavior. If we have the right goals, we may very well have the right behavior. Paul said that he did one thing—he pressed forward toward the goal: "Not that I have already obtained, or am already made perfect: but I press on, if so be that I may lay hold on that for which also I was laid hold on by Christ Jesus. Brethren, I count not myself yet to have laid hold: but one thing I do, forgetting the things which are behind, and stretching forward to the things which are before, I press on toward the goal unto the prize of the high calling of God in Christ Jesus."

Abraham and Sarah had the goal of a house not made with hands. In Hebrews 11:8–11 we read: "By faith Abraham, when he was called, obeyed to go out unto a place which he was to receive for an inheritance; and he went out, not knowing whither he went. By faith he became a sojourner in the land of promise, as in a land not his own, dwelling in tents, with Isaac and Jacob, the heirs with him of the same promise: for he looked for the city which hath the foundations, whose builder and maker is God. By faith even Sarah herself received power to conceive seed when she was past age, since she counted him faithful who had promised." These people knew what they really wanted in life. They knew where to look for eternal happiness.

We should have *worthy* goals. I would like to suggest some:
• We should strive to live the right kind of example for others. In Matthew 5:16 we read: "Even so let your light shine before men; that they may see your good works, and glorify your Father who is in heaven." If we lead others in the wrong direction, our lives are not successful.
• We should plan to marry for life. The idea of trial marriage is not found in the Bible. The Bible condemned the putting away of women. Micah 2:9, for instance, says: "The women of my people ye cast out from their pleasant houses; from their young children ye take away my glory for ever." Jesus spoke against divorce in Matthew 19:8–9: "He saith unto them, Moses for your hardness of heart suffered you to put away your wives: but from the beginning it hath not been so. And I say unto you, Whosoever shall put away his wife except for fornication, and shall marry another, committeth adultery: and he that marrieth her when she is put away committeth adultery." Previously, in Matthew 5:31–32, Jesus had said: "It was said also, Whosoever shall put away his wife, let him give her a writing of divorcement, but, I say unto you, that everyone that putteth away his wife, saving for the cause of fornication, maketh her an adulteress: and whosoever shall marry her when she is put away committeth adultery." Therefore, marriage should not be entered into lightly but reverently and in the fear of the Lord. It

should be entered into with the idea of staying together for life. This is the proper goal for couples to have.
• Another worthy goal is for both husband and wife to be Christians. If they are not, they will not have the same goals and will not be able to grow together in every aspect of their intimate relationship as they could if they were Christians. It is still very difficult for two to walk together unless they agree. For those who have been able to get along in marriage when they were not both Christians, we are thankful, but they usually admit that their situation is not ideal, that they could be happier if both partners were Christians. The general principle along these lines is found in II Corinthians 6:14: "Be not unequally yoked with unbelievers: for what fellowship have righteousness and iniquity? Or what communion hath light with darkness?" When two are not agreed in religion, they are more likely to argue over matters of morals and principles than they are when both are Christians.
• Another goal for the home is peace of mind. We should want to have peace with God. Jesus said that he left his peace with us. During the last week of his life, recorded in John 14:27, we find this attitude expressed by Jesus in the following words: "Peace I leave with you; my peace I give unto you. Let not your heart be troubled, neither let it be fearful." Peace between the husband and wife, between the parents and children, should also be a goal. We should be at peace in the family and not at war. When people are always fussing in the home, it is not a happy home. Jesus said in Matthew 5:9: "Blessed are the peacemakers: for they shall be called sons of God." Are you a peacemaker in the home or a peacebreaker?
• We should want to go to heaven. Every member in the family should try to help every other member in the family go to heaven. Jesus has gone to prepare a place for us, and he will come again to receive us unto himself (John 14:1–6). If we do not live the kind of Christian life we should live, we may very well influence some member of the family to be lost eternally. Mark Twain's wife was a "Christian" when they first married. They often prayed and read the Bible together. However, one night he asked her to pray. She answered that she could not do so because he had led her away from her faith. He was not a Christian. In fact, he often ridiculed religion. That statement she

made bothered him for the rest of his life. What if someone said to one of us, "You have led me from my faith"? This would probably bother us for the rest of our lives. Thus, we ought to live in such a way as to try to help others strengthen their faith so that they may be saved eternally.

Behavior

A number of mistakes made in the home might be characterized as "wrong behavior." In fact, goals and behavior really tell the story of what goes on in life and in the home.

Husbands and Wives

Most surveys of marriage counselors indicate that the majority of marital problems fall into three categories: money, sex, and in-laws. I would like to add a fourth—religion.

Problems with money usually center around arguments over how it is spent. Sometimes the wife is accustomed to higher living standards than her husband can provide. She may spend more than the husband earns. This, of course, causes problems. Another problem exists when both husband and wife desire material things too much. They may both work and devote all their energies to making money without thinking of other important aspects of their relationship.

Another matter relating to money is often very serious. The husband may be the breadwinner in the home and thus think that all the money he earns is his. He may then give his wife an allowance much as he would a child. He does not think that part of the money actually belongs to the wife, although she works in the home and does her part just as he works at his job to make the money for the family. When only the husband works, he should think of the money as belonging to both the husband and the wife. It is part hers because she is doing what she has been assigned to do in the home. She is carrying her part of the load. Basically the problem is selfishness. If neither partner is selfish, there should be no problems with money. If either is selfish, there will be problems with money that may destroy the relationship between the husband and the wife.

Various problems might be discussed under the label of sex.

Either the husband or the wife may be cold toward the other and not want to have anything to do with the other as husband or wife. Sometimes a person gets married and thinks he can continue to live as he did before he was married. The person continues to think of sex in the same way as he did before he was married. However, the Bible says in Hebrews 13:4 that the marriage bed is to be undefiled. There is nothing wrong with sex in marriage. We also read in I Corinthians 7 that each is to give the other his due. Such problems as uncleanliness, fatigue, and excessive overweight may cause sex problems. Attractiveness is a necessary element in the marriage relationship.

Problems with sex may be a symptom of other problems. If the husband and wife do not love each other, they will probably have sex problems. Often sex problems are very, very real. For example, one thirty-six-year-old woman told a preacher that she and her husband had not lived together as husband and wife for five years. She then blamed her husband for running off and marrying another woman. Both she and her husband were guilty.

Disloyalty is a very serious problem. Sometimes one or both members of the husband-wife team may be disloyal and commit adultery. This invariably breaks up the home. The Bible says that fornicators shall not inherit the kingdom of God (I Cor. 6:9-10). Disloyalty is one of the greatest sins against a happy home. Very few homes stay together and maintain happiness when disloyalty occurs.

Another problem related to sex is birth control. Some people in the church still believe that birth control is wrong, that sex somehow is sinful unless it is related to procreation. However, in I Corinthians 7 we learn that one of the purposes of marriage is to prevent fornication. The sex drive is real. Many psychologists say that it is second only to hunger and thirst in its urgency. Sex is the character of being either male or female. We should all remember that God created sex (Gen. 1).

The third big problem between husbands and wives is the problem of in-laws. At times in-laws divide the husband and wife. This sometimes happens early in their marriage. The husband, for example, may go to his relatives and tell them his side of any controversy with his wife. They usually take sides with him. This reinforces him against his wife. The wife may also go to her family and tell her side of the story. They then usually take sides with her. This solidifies the wife in her position against the husband. Because of such matters, it is possibly a good idea for the husband and wife to live a number of miles away from their relatives for a few years after they get married. Usually if they can get along well for two or three years after they are married, the in-laws will not be such a big problem after that.

Often the in-laws do not understand the context of a discussion that went on between a husband and wife. They are also very much prejudiced and do not see both sides. It is hard for in-laws not to comment about things that are very important to the husband and wife, things they need to settle for themselves, such as methods and principles of child-rearing.

Religion may also be a problem with husbands and wives. If they do not agree in religion, it can become a point of division in their marriage instead of a point of unification. Morals are part of religion. What is right or wrong? How do we rear the children? Why can't we go to church together? How much do we give the church? How do we go about discussing religion with our friends? All of these points are hard to discuss when the husband and wife differ in their religious views.

Young people ought to give serious consideration to these matters before they are married. Often when I have preached, urging young people to marry a Christian, I have been a little reluctant for fear of hurting the feelings of someone in the audience who has married a non-Christian. Usually, however, the person in the audience who has married outside his faith will come to me later and tell me that I was right and that I should not be so reluctant to urge young people to marry people who have a similar faith. One lady recently told me, "You just don't know how rough it is, what I have been through over the years!" I have talked to many members of the church who have married outside their faith. Most have had numerous problems. Religion can be a unifying force or a dividing force in the home. Young people should weigh this matter very carefully before they are married.

Parents

Parents sometimes behave in the wrong way. For example, their own emotional problems can cause problems for their children. They may make the child an escape for their own problems. Some psychologists say that there is a "need" in some emotionally disturbed families for a schizophrenic child. They force a child into schizophrenic behavior in order to satisfy their own needs.

Each family has certain patterns of interaction. As a person changes, others in the family also change. A neurotic person often associates with those with whom he can maintain his actions. Family interactions help determine abnormal as well as normal behavior. The study of the family homeostasis is a study of a balance of the various roles each member plays in the family. If you change one role, other roles are also affected. Some families may have a role for one member of the family that requires that person to be schizophrenic. Some families may even expect one member of the family to be dishonest by the way they treat him. The family may even play a certain game— the "if it weren't for you, I would be all right" game. "I am adequate; it is because of you that things are going wrong." When the family finally finds homeostasis, they may be forcing the child into undesirable behavior. He may be forced, for example, to withdraw and say nothing in order to keep family homeostasis or balance. He may then be unable to cope with others and be considered schizophrenic.

Many authorities think that parents are the cause of juvenile delinquency. The child is the delinquent, but the parents may be the cause because they have not adequately taught the child. Perhaps the problem is due to the fact that the parents have no real morals or do not have an adequate relationship with the child. Many authorities today think that the sociopath or the psychopath is conditioned to play that role by his parents. There is open rejection of the child by the parents, most often by the father. If the father rejects the child, the mother may try to make up for this. Usually they are both permissive, and one parent works against the other. The child is openly rejected by one or both parents. They do not love him or accept him no matter what he does. The child then grows up without learning how to love.

In normal development the child accepts the values of the parents. A sociopath never picks up the parents' values. Thus, he never accepts society's values. He accepts only his own values. The child first does not accept the parents; then he tries to get even with the parents and later with society by antisocial behavior. Thus, Scripture is right in teaching that parents should love their children and give guidance to them. In fact, discipline is not very effective when administered by someone who is hated.

Children

We are told in the Bible that children should obey their parents in the Lord (Eph. 6:1). Children and young people should look upon obedience to parents as an obligation when such obedience does not necessitate disobedience to God. Parents should see their great responsibility to live the right kind of lives and to administer discipline in the right way. Children must follow parents. Children who are not disciplined by parents will most likely be unable later on in life to lead well-ordered lives. They may not be able to put the brakes on themselves. Cars and children must have brakes as well as motors. The Bible teaches us to put brakes on the following basic drives:

1. *Pride.* A man may think so highly of himself that he almost thinks of himself as being God. To such a man Paul wrote, "For I say, through the grace that was given me, to every man that is among you, not to think of himself more highly than he ought to think; but so to think as to think soberly, according as God hath dealt to each man a measure of faith" (Rom. 12:8). In another passage this same apostle warned us, saying, "For who maketh thee to differ? and what hast thou that thou didst not receive? but if thou didst receive it, why dost thou glory as if thou hadst not received it?" (I Cor. 4:7).

2. *Selfishness.* In reference to this problem, Christ said, "If any man would come after me, let him deny himself, and take up his cross, and follow me" (Matt. 16:24). Later he taught that if anyone would be a minister, he must be a servant (Matt. 20:26–28).

3. *Greed.* Jesus said in reference to greed, "Lay not up for yourselves treasures upon the earth, where moth and rust consume, and where thieves break through and steal; but lay up for yourselves treasures in heaven, where neither moth nor rust doth consume, and where thieves do not break through nor steal: for where thy treasure is, there will thy heart be also" (Matt. 6:19–21). Later he said that a man's life does not consist in the abundance of his possessions (Luke 12:15).

4. *Hatred.* With reference to attitudes such as hatred, resentment, and jealousy, Jesus said, "Ye have heard that it was said to them of old time, Thou shalt not kill; and whosoever shall kill shall be in danger of the judgment; but I say unto you that everyone who is angry with his brother shall be in danger of the hell of fire" (Matt. 5:21–22). He further said that if someone hits you on one cheek to turn the other also (Matt. 5:38–39).

5. *Lust.* The Bible also teaches that we must put our brakes on lust. With reference to this point, Jesus said, "Ye have heard that it was said, Thou shalt not commit adultery; but everyone that looketh on a woman to lust after her hath committed adultery with her already in his heart" (Matt. 5:27–28). Paul commanded that we must keep ourselves clean from all defilement of flesh and spirit, perfecting holiness in the fear of God (II Cor. 6:17–7:1). Obedience to parents in the name of the Lord will help children to be obedient to God, to practice self-discipline in every sphere of their lives. As adults they will be more inclined to live well-ordered, happy, disciplined lives in the fear of the Lord.

Positive Principles

The following positive principles will help the Christian have a happier home life.

First of all, there is the principle expressed in Scripture that we ought to be willing to give ourselves away. This principle goes against the fleshly nature of man. We fight such ideas. Even the apostle Peter opposed Jesus when Jesus suggested that he was going to the cross (Matt. 16:22). But Jesus did not agree with Peter. In fact, he called Peter "Satan" because Peter opposed his efforts to give himself on the cross (Matt. 16:23). Jesus wants us to give ourselves for others, to serve them.

Second Peter 1:5–7 establishes some very important biblical principles for the home. This passage reads, "And beside this, giving all diligence, add to your faith virtue; and to virtue knowledge; and to knowledge temperance; and to temperance patience; and to patience godliness; and to godliness brotherly kindness; and to brotherly kindness charity." Such principles as these will help our homes to be what they ought to be.

The principle of trust is also very important. We must learn to trust God when things are not going the way we would like them to go. In Philippians 4:4–7 Paul said, "Rejoice in the Lord always: again I will say, Rejoice. Let your forbearance be known unto all men. The Lord is at hand. In nothing be anxious; but in everything by prayer and supplication with thanksgiving let your requests be made known unto God. And the peace of God, which passeth all understanding, shall guard your hearts and your thoughts in Christ Jesus." May we be willing to give ourselves for others, to build the kind of Christian character that God outlines for us in the Bible, and to place our trust completely in God. This will enable us to build on our mistakes, to correct them, and to have the kind of homes that please God. May God bless us toward this end.

QUESTIONS FOR DISCUSSION

1. Discuss some biblical examples of unhappy homes.
2. What goals lead to unhappy homes?
3. If you were doing it all over again, what sorts of things in your prospective mate would indicate trouble ahead?
4. How do you know when a marriage is in trouble?
5. How can you tell when someone else's children are developing improperly? What are some signs of trouble ahead?
6. How much has our culture influenced our concept of husband-wife relationships?
7. Read I Peter 3:1-7 and discuss how it applies to marriage today.

11

The Happy Home

In the autumn of 1822, after nine years in Paris, a certain American playwright was very lonely. Being absent from home for such a long period, this man, John Howard Payne, became very homesick. He sat down at his desk and wrote, "Mid pleasures and palaces though we may roam, be it ever so humble, there is no place like home." One year later, the song was sung in London. The singer, Maria Tree, received a standing ovation. Twenty-seven years later, Jenny Lind, a world-famous singer, appeared in a concert in Washington. Many dignitaries, including the President of the United States, were present. Daniel Webster stood and bowed toward the singer. After acknowledging this courtesy, Jenny Lind turned and faced a man who was seated inconspicuously in the hall. She did not take her eyes off him as she sang "Home, Sweet Home." Tears began to run down Payne's face. At the end of the song it would have been difficult to have found a dry eye in the entire audience.

Even if you do not believe in the magic of words, there is a tremendous power in the words *home* and *family*. "Home is where the heart is," is a statement going back all the way to Pliny, a Roman statesman and scholar who was a contemporary of Christ's apostles. Biblical teachings on the family will help produce happy and useful lives. Many families today are not what they ought to be. They often are divided emotionally as well as physically. In some families the entire family does not eat even one meal together. When the riots broke out in the Watts district of Los Angeles, it was discovered that many of the families were without a father in the home. The father had deserted the rest of the family. Divorce and remarriage are

103

sanctioned more today than ever before. For these and other reasons we need to study what the Bible says about the family.

The family holds society together like a rope—each thread in the rope has its place in holding the rope together as each family in society has its place in holding society together. Marriage has reached a turning point when we read of mate swapping, free sex, and polygamy. Thirty-four percent of those responding in a 1971 survey said that marriage is obsolete. The institution of marriage is first mentioned in the Bible in Genesis 1:27–28: "And God created man in his own image, in the image of God created he him; male and female created he them. And God blessed them and God said unto them, Be fruitful, and multiply, and replenish the earth, and subdue it; and have dominion over the fish of the sea, and over the birds of the heavens, and over every living thing that moveth upon the earth." The specific story of the creation of woman is found in Genesis 2:18 where we read: "And Jehovah God said, It is not good that the man should be alone; I will make him a help meet for him." So out of man came woman, and God brought her unto the man. "And the man said, This is now bone of my bones, and flesh of my flesh; she shall be called Woman because she was taken out of man" (Gen. 2:23). The next verse says, "Therefore shall a man leave his father and his mother, and shall cleave unto his wife: and they shall be one flesh."

There are certain provisions for the happy family. The needs of the various members of the family are provided by the home. What are some of these basic needs?

The Need for Closeness

People don't like to feel isolated. One of the needs often expressed by people is the need for fellowship with others. In the happy family no one should be lonely. Every member of the family should feel that he is in close fellowship with every other member of the family. Children should feel close to each other and to their parents, and parents should feel close to each other and to their children.

Marriage is a union between a man and a woman. Other things are implied, but certainly the physical union is included. Two become one flesh. It is amazing that Christians still feel

guilty about sex after they are married. The Bible plainly says
that sex in marriage is approved by God. One Christian lady
said that she asked God to forgive her after she had been intimate with her husband. No wonder a lot of marriages break up.
Couples should not feel guilty when they are intimate with each
other. The bed is to be undefiled (Heb. 13:4).

We are told in I Peter 3:7, "Ye husbands, in like manner, dwell
with your wives according to knowledge, giving honor unto the
woman, as unto the weaker vessel, as being also joint-heirs of
the grace of life; to the end that your prayers be not hindered."
Couples should know certain things about each other's needs.
They should study and learn as much as they can about each
other. Some husbands do not know, for example, that their
wives are unable to separate sex and love in their minds and in
their hearts. For the husband these two are more easily sepa-
rated, generally speaking, than for the wife.

Knowledge about a number of things can help the husband
and wife to be close to each other. They are to be aware of the
needs of each other, physical needs as well as other needs
(I Cor. 7:1-5). In Genesis 3 God told Eve that her desire would be
to her husband (Gen. 3:16). Thus, God does not say that desire
is wrong in marriage. In the Song of Solomon, the husband has
desire for the wife. There is attraction between a country girl and
a shepherd boy. Earlier in the Old Testament, Rachel was beautiful and attractive to Jacob. This is a part of God's plan in bringing man and woman together. Jacob was so attracted to Rachel
that he served fourteen years for her, and these years seemed
but a few days. Nothing is said in Scripture to condemn Jacob's
attraction to Rachel. Sex is the total alliance between two persons. This togetherness and closeness become a core of the marriage relationship.

There are certain *pillars* that undergird closeness in marriage. Permanence in the family relationship is one of these pillars. We are told that we are to leave father and mother and
cleave to our spouse. If we are here today and gone tomorrow,
we cannot build up any sort of closeness with our marriage
partner.

Another pillar is preeminence. The marriage relationship is
preeminent over all other relationships. Father and mother are
not to be more important than wife or husband. No previous
close friend is to be as important as the mate. One couple who

put their marriage first said, "If we were not Christians, we would get a divorce. But by God's grace we will make it." They were giving marriage a preeminent place in their lives.

Because we are close in the happy family, we can be ourselves in the home more than we can in any other place. If we cannot, something is wrong. The home is the place for regeneration for each member of the family. This is the place where we do not have to wear a mask, where we can "let our hair down." This is a place where each member of the family is loved and accepted for what he is. Each member of the family enjoys the company of other members of the family. This fellowship helps satisfy emotional needs.

The Need for Love

Many psychologists say today that mental illness is the inability of a person to give or take love. Much of therapy is designed to repair damages that have isolated a person emotionally from others. The home helps fulfill the need of each person for love. Ephesians 5:23–28 commands us to love one another. Each member of the family should love one another. How much should the husband love his wife? As Christ loved the church. As he loves himself. As he loves his own body.

Dr. Hugo McCord offered to give one of his eyes to his wife so that she could continue to see. This is a good illustration of the kind of love discussed in Ephesians 5. How long should the husband love his wife? As long as Christ loves the church. He does not quit loving the church but will love the church throughout the ages. The husband should love his wife until death. In Romans 7:2 we read, "For the woman that hath a husband is bound by law to the husband while he liveth; but if the husband die, she is discharged from the law of the husband." The writer further says that if the wife marries another man while the husband is alive, she is an adulteress (Rom. 7:3). Jesus basically taught the same principle of permanence in Matthew 5:32 when he said, "But I say unto you that everyone that putteth away his wife, saving for the cause of fornication, maketh her an adulteress; and whosoever shall marry her when she is put away committeth adultery." The husband should not stop loving his wife for any reason. He took her for better or for worse. The same is true of the wife's love for her husband. She took him "until death do us part."

Love never fails (I Cor. 13:4–8). In fact, love is the emotion that motivates the entire Christian life. It is a wonderful thing when each member of the family loves every other member. When people can grow old together, loving each other, life becomes meaningful and beautiful. It is a lot easier to live that way. This idea is similar to the lines in Robert Browning's poem, "Rabbi Ben Ezra."

> Grow old along with me, the best is yet to be
> The last of life for which the first was made.

When we love each other, we can grow together as we grow older. The years sweeten the relationship. Love helps us to forget the infirmities of the flesh.

The Need for Discipline

Discipline is a word that is not used much today. However, we just cannot do without it. Children cannot grow up and live well-ordered lives without discipline. This discipline is provided by Christian parents. Children must learn how to live at home. Parents must take a firm stand to give values to children. Their lives are then ordered by the values they hold.

Our heavenly Father has given us permanent values and truths. We read in John 12:48, "He that rejecteth me, and receiveth not my sayings, hath one that judgeth him: the word that I spake, the same shall judge him in the last day." We will be judged according to certain principles and commands whether we have been taught them or not. They do not change from year to year. Parents need to love their children. They need to be consistent as much as possible. They need to, as Paul said in Ephesians 6:4, "provoke not your children to wrath; but nurture them in the chastening and admonition of the Lord." They need to see that love demands discipline and guidance.

One mother was mistaken in her attitude when she said, "I can't tell my child no because I love him too much." This is not love. Letting a child eat what he wants to eat, read what he wants to read, see what he wants to see, go out with whom he wishes to go out, and go to bed when he wishes to go to bed is not love. This is actually the easy way out of parental responsibility. We may not want to have any conflict with the child because we personally do not like conflict. We need to stand for certain principles as parents, even if these principles lead to conflict. Why? Because we love our children. We want them not only to have a nice day but also to have a nice eternity. We want them to live well-ordered, useful, disciplined lives in this world and to be happy in the world to come.

The Need for Peace

Every person has a need for peace: peace with God, peace with self, and peace with others. This peace must start in the home. If a person does not experience peace in the home, he will probably be very unhappy in his life and may be very unsettled emotionally. The character of each home should include peace and contentment. We should not have to be on guard with other members of the family. We should not have to watch every word that we say for fear that it will be taken in the wrong way.

Attitudes make up the character of the home. These attitudes are very important motivators. Take, for example, Peter's actions against the Gentiles in Galatians 2:11–16. He knew intellectually what was right, but emotionally he reacted against the Gentiles and acted in a sinful way because his attitude toward them was wrong. We learn attitudes in the home. Illustrations of attitudes are such things as prejudice, hostility, anger, love, and concern. Such an attitude as peace of mind is more caught than taught. We teach by example and by the general atmosphere that is found in the home. These are definite causative factors of children's attitudes. A judgmental person usually does not have peace of mind. He is always ready to condemn other people. He is not at peace with himself, and this is the reason he condemns others. He, in fact, may be dishonest as he judges others. He may be projecting his own inadequacies onto them. How tragic when parents are this way!

Jesus said in Matthew 7:1–5: "Judge not, that ye be not judged. For with what judgment ye judge, ye shall be judged: and with what measure ye mete, it shall be measured unto you. And why beholdest thou the mote that is in thy brother's eye, but considereth not the beam that is in thine own eye? Or how wilt thou say to thy brother, Let me cast out the mote out of thine eye; and lo, the beam is in thine own eye? Thou hypocrite, cast out first the beam out of thine own eye; and then shalt thou see clearly to cast out the mote out of thy brother's eye." Often when a person judges another, it is because he knows that he has committed the same sins. Paul recognized this when he said in Romans 2:3: "And reckonest thou this, O man, who judgest them that practise such things and doest the same, that thou shalt escape the judgment of God?"

We must be at peace with ourselves, with others, and with God. Jesus demanded that we become peacemakers in Matthew 5:9: "Blessed are the peacemakers: for they shall be called sons of God." Peace is lacking in many homes. People are on the defensive with each other. They cannot loosen up and have close fellowship with the family.

The place to start is with self and with God. Get right with God and with self, and then you can see more clearly how to be right with others. Your family needs this kind of atmosphere in your home.

The Need for Conversion to Christ

Each member of the family needs to be Christian. Real Christianity makes a difference in the home. Not too long ago a man named Jack Wyrtzen debated the atheist Madalyn Murray O'Hair on the radio. He said that he was clearly losing the debate until a teenager called in and gave her story. She said, "A year ago, Mrs. O'Hair, I was failing in all my subjects in high school, a potential dropout. My life was a chaos of rebellion and delinquency. I was desperately unhappy, but I met Christ. Now I have peace, and I am on the honor roll at school and expect to graduate soon. Mrs. O'Hair, what would atheism have to offer a young person in the condition I was in a year ago?" After this call Mr. Wyrtzen said that he began to win the debate. This was the turning point in his discussion with this atheist. A Christian home must uphold Jesus Christ. This really makes a difference.

Dr. Thomas Campbell of California recently made the statement that the churches in the Southwest have failed in efforts to build up congregations because they have taken the approach of bringing children to the services but not parents. Children should be brought to the services, but his point was that we must also reach the parents if the church is to be stable and if we are to keep the children when they grow up. We need the cooperation of the homes. Experience teaches us that this is true. A number of congregations around the country attest to this fact. Often teenagers come to church without their parents. But usually when they get to be about seventeen years old, many of them discontinue their church attendance and leave the faith. We need the entire family working together to influence each to stay with Christ.

Homes without a sense of morality do not please God. Sodom could have been saved had there been ten godly homes within its gates (Gen. 19). Homes today without Christ are not models to follow. For example, a recent survey indicated 40 percent of all girls have had sexual relations before eighteen. Many couples are living together without the benefit of marriage. One girl who was brought up in the South recently was found living in a commune in California. She said that she had never really been converted to Christ. She did not feel that other family members in her home were converted to the Lord, although they went to all of the church services.

Real conversion can lead to a feeling of security. Parents take the responsibility that God has given them. They provide both spiritually and physically for the members of the family (I Tim. 5:8). They emphasize sharing responsibilities in the home. Each family member has his own responsibilities. Some of these responsibilities are outlined in the following Bible passages. In I Timothy 5:14 we read, "I desire therefore that the younger widows marry, bear children, rule the household, give no occasion to the adversary for reviling." Paul outlines the role of the woman in the home in Titus 2:1–5, "But speak thou the things which befit the sound doctrine: that aged men be temperate, grave, sober-minded, sound in faith, in love, in patience: that aged women likewise be reverent in demeanor, not slanderers nor enslaved to much wine, teachers of that which is good; that they may train the young women to love their husbands, to love their children, to be sober-minded, chaste, workers at home, kind, being in subjection to their own husbands, that the word of God be not blasphemed." In Ephesians 5 we learn that the husband is to be the head of the family and the wife is to love her husband. In Romans 1:28–30 we read that when people fall away from God their children will be disobedient to their parents. Obedience to parents is also taught in a positive way in Ephesians 6:1–3 and in other places. For example, when Jesus was twelve years old he was said to be subject to his parents (Luke 2:51). When each person carries out his own responsibilities in the home and is converted to the Lord, this helps to give stability and a sense of security to each member of the family. The goal of Christian parents is to meet the needs of the family.

The Need for Communication

People feel isolated and lonely on many occasions. They feel the need to really talk to someone. One of the amazing things we have found out in the last few years is that it is possible for a person to live in a big city and still feel very lonely. Sometimes even in the home people do not really communicate with each other. They feel lonely. Lines of communication must be kept open. If such lines are not kept open, the problem is not usually communication but something else.

We need to talk to each other. We need to be willing to listen to each member of the family. Sometimes certain families have one or more members of the family that they just do not listen to at all. Sometimes it is father, sometimes it is mother, and often it is the children. We cannot communicate unless we listen.

Conclusions

An unusual experience was reported by Admiral Richard E. Byrd. During his first expedition to the South Pole, Admiral Byrd was temporarily isolated from other members of the expedition. One day he was lost in a sudden blizzard. There was nothing in the barren whiteness to give him a sense of direction. He knew if he just struck out blindly to find his hut that he would get lost and would freeze to death in the storm. He took a pole that he had in his hand to use in feeling for holes in the ice and stuck it in the snow and tied a scarf around it so he could see the pole for a certain distance. He then took several trips, looking for his hut. Three times he failed. Each time he returned to the center and tried again. He said that without his pole serving as center, he would have died in the storm. As I think about the family, I think of it as being a center. We go out into the world from this center. We find God from this center. We relate to others from this center. If the home is what it ought to be, we will have a real sense of guidance and stability from which to radiate.

A home should provide for the various needs of each member of the family. These include the need for closeness, for love, for discipline, for peace, for conversion to Christ, and for communication. If the family is what it ought to be, these needs will be met, and each member of the family will have a center of stability and importance from which to live his life.

QUESTIONS FOR DISCUSSION

1. What does the word "home" mean to you?
2. Discuss some happy homes in the Bible.
3. What individual needs should be met in the home?
4. Read Gen. 1:26-27, Gen. 2:18-24, and Eph. 5:22-6:4 and discuss foundations for the home that are presented.
5. How would you discipline a 15-year-old child differently from a six-year-old child?
6. Are there gender differences in discipline methods?
7. What makes a home happy, healthy, and Christian?

12

The Christian Personality

Many people appreciate the Sermon on the Mount. Scholars declare it to be one of the world's greatest pieces of literature. For believers in Christ it contains the heart of Christ's teaching and is, in a real sense, the constitution of the Christian faith.

The Sermon on the Mount describes the citizens of the kingdom. Christians are told how to live (Matt. 5–7).

The Poor in Spirit

Jesus said, "Blessed are the poor in spirit: for theirs is the kingdom of heaven." The word *blessed* means happy, an inner peace and happiness that has little correlation with outward circumstances. It continues to sustain one even under difficult circumstances.

Jesus says that we must be poor in spirit as we begin our journey to spiritual maturity and happiness. He did not say we have to be poor in order to be saved, but that we must be poor in spirit. Our attitude must be one of humility before we can expect God to come into our lives.

To be poor in spirit does not mean to be pessimistic. Many pessimistic people are not poor in spirit. To be poor in spirit is to deny one's self. The word Jesus uses for "poor" is a very strong word for poverty, a word that means *"beggar."* To be utterly poor in spirit, a person must feel that he is destitute without God.

"Blessed are the poor in spirit: for theirs is the kingdom of heaven." Only humble people would enter the kingdom! Jesus said, "Except ye turn, and become as little children, ye shall in no wise enter into the kingdom of heaven" (Matt. 18:3). Without humility we are of no use to God. Peter serves as an example. He once told Jesus that even the threat of death would not cause him to be unfaithful. Later Peter learned the lesson of humility and "became poor in spirit." This led to his forgiveness. When Jesus asked Peter to feed his sheep, Peter did not brag at all. Nor did he compare his faithfulness with others. He had learned that one must be poor in spirit to be of service in the kingdom of God (Matt. 26–27; John 21).

Jesus came as a servant. He did not come to show his greatness but to serve. Pride can keep us from becoming Christians. We can be too proud to bend to the commands of God. We can be too proud to see the good in other people. We can be too proud to forgive others.

Those Who Mourn

"Blessed are they that mourn: for they shall be comforted." The person who mourns is not only sorry for his sin but is grieved because of it. He mourns because he has sinned and because others have sinned. Peter became poor in spirit when he realized that he had sinned against Jesus. He mourned because of his sin, and he was comforted. Had he remained proud he could not have served the church at all. We must be deeply grieved when we sin.

The Meek

"Blessed are the meek: for they shall inherit the earth." It is easy to imagine that the people who heard Jesus were very surprised at what he said. They did not believe a meek man would inherit anything. Neither do people today. We do not visualize a meek man succeeding at anything. We believe him to be too weak. But weakness is not meekness. The word *meek* in the Greek language is the same as the word used for "an animal that is domesticated." A meek animal is one that has been tamed, an animal that obeys his master's voice. A meek man then is a God-tamed man, a man who is ready to leave self and accept

God. He is domesticated by God. Thus the passage could be translated, "Blessed is the God-tamed person."

God rules over the lives of the people who make up his kingdom. Moses was a man with tremendous power. But he was a meek man, a God-tamed man, domesticated for God's service. He listened to God and was controlled by God. Jesus is the perfect example of meekness. He said of himself, "I am meek and lowly in heart" (Matt. 11:28–30). He completely surrendered his will to God's will. We are on the road to God when we reach the point of surrendering our will to his. This is true meekness.

Those Who Hunger and Thirst

The fourth beatitude of Matthew 5 is, "Blessed are they that hunger and thirst after righteousness: for they shall be filled." The person described here desires righteousness. The fact that a person hungers and thirsts after righteousness indicates that he is on his way toward God.

It is hard for most of us to appreciate the meaning of the word *hunger*. Many people in the days of Jesus had been hungry— they knew what it meant. The average person of that day ate meat only once a week. They knew what it was to be hungry.

What about being thirsty? Since we have plenty of water, most of us do not know what it means to be thirsty. Perhaps we have been out in the field a few times without water and have become thirsty, but this is only for a few hours. Such experiences, however, give us some knowledge of thirst. Sometimes in Palestinian deserts, dust storms would drive people to cover their mouths and cause them to become extremely thirsty. Once a man became so thirsty that he said to himself, "I would give my right arm for a drink of water." Later, being even more thirsty, he said, "I'd give both of my arms for a drink of water." Finally, his thirst was so intense that he cried, "I'd give my life for a drink of water. I'd die right now for a drink of water." Jesus was saying, "Blessed is the person who really wants to do what is right, who desires a full measure of righteousness." A Christian must want to be completely right; he must accept all of God's will. He must desire to do what God wants him to do. Such a person has life.

The first step on the road to Christian maturity is to leave self and to desire righteousness. Then there is room for Christ. Are we like this?

The Merciful

Describing the Christian personality, Jesus said, "Blessed are the merciful: for they shall obtain mercy." Mercy has to do with being willing to forgive people. I've seen people who have been forgiven, but have in the process been trodden under the feet of those forgiving them. This is not the kind of forgiveness Jesus is talking about. Real forgiveness is willingness to be generous and to show pity. The characteristic of true pity is to take positive action when a person needs our help. For example, we read of the good Samaritan who helped a person in need. He showed mercy to him. This is the kind of mercy that Jesus is talking about here—a positive kind of mercy. When a Christian sees a person in need and has pity on him, he shows kindness toward that person. He is becoming Christlike in the positive action that he takes.

It takes a lot of big people to keep things going in the world. We need people who have Christlike characteristics and who think, "Well, I am just the way I am because I am of Christ; I am not looking for any special glory or praise, and I don't expect people to praise me every time I do a good deed. "The merciful shall obtain mercy. "For judgment is without mercy to him that hath showed no mercy" (James 2:13).

The Pure in Heart

Jesus also said, "Blessed are the pure in heart: for they shall see God." When we think of purity, we think of someone who has not sinned. A person who is pure in heart is a person who has a single heart. He has one motive in his life. This is the basic meaning of the word *purity* here. It is a word that means "single"—having a single motive.

We talk a lot about pollution. Pollution is an antonym for purity. To be polluted is to be impure. If you mix anything with that which is pure, it is not pure anymore. The Christian heart is not hypocritical. It is a heart with a single purpose in mind, not a polluted heart with different purposes. Jesus expressed the same thought when he said, "You cannot serve both God and mammon" (Matt. 6:24). We try to go one way part of the time and another way part of the time, but the person who has a pure heart is not selfish; he is not hypocritical in his motives; he serves God because of the motive of wanting to please his heavenly Father. Such service is not to get glory; a real Christian serves because he wants to please God. This is the overriding motive of the Christian's life.

The Peacemakers

Jesus also said, "Blessed are the peacemakers: for they shall be called the children of God." When we think of peace, we usually think of the absence of trouble, and this is a necessary part of the definition of peace: the absence of fighting, quarreling, and ill feeling. Peacemakers harbor neither hatred nor ill will toward others. Wishing another peace means, "May everything that is good in the world, all the blessings of God, be upon you." Peace is the absence of trouble, but it is also a positive good. The person who is a peacemaker does everything good that he can. Everything that would make for peace, anything that would make for the well-being of people—is what a Christian does. If he is a real peacemaker, he will not just settle quarrels but will do whatever adds to the common good of people. He brings harmony to the world. He influences the world for good.

When we think of peace, we think first of all of peace with God. This is part of the peace which Jesus was talking about here. We certainly are not peacemakers if we are not at peace with God. There is no peace for the wicked (Isa. 57:20-21). We must surrender to God's will. We must have the right motive and purpose in serving God. We must hunger and thirst after righteousness. We must desire righteousness above all else.

When we are at peace with God, then we can be peacemakers in the world. God's people go out with joy and are led forth with peace (Isa. 55:12). We can bring this peace of God to those around us. Complete peace also means peace with other people. We should try to be at peace with all men. Such peace is desperately needed in the world today. It takes a big person to be a peacemaker.

The word *peace* not only has to do with peace with God and peace with people but also peace with self. Such peace is needed in the world today—to be willing to accept ourselves, to be able to like ourselves, and to be at peace with ourselves. It is a wonderful thing to be able to look at one's self and not be ashamed. In trying to be at peace with God, with self, and with others, one is following a conscience which is guided by the Word of God. Soon that person will have the peace of God that "passeth all understanding"—the most wonderful thing a person can possess.

There is no easy road to Christian happiness. It involves being poor in spirit, being willing to submit ourselves to God's will, having a singleness of heart and purpose in life. All of these divine characteristics come from God. The greatest mercy one can know comes from God. When one thinks about purity, one thinks about God in whom there is no hypocrisy. When one thinks about peacemaking, one thinks of Jesus, the Prince of peace. God wants us to be at peace—with ourselves, with him, and with each other.

The Persecuted

The eighth beatitude of Matthew 5 teaches us to be strong enough to endure persecution. The mature Christian person who has truly lost self is willing to follow Jesus even to the point of being persecuted for righteousness' sake. Any person who is weak as a Christian may be easily discouraged when things do not go exactly right. Such a person may conclude that Christianity is not worth anything at all. But the person who has Christlike characteristics becomes strong with the help of God. "Blessed are they who are persecuted for righteousness' sake: for theirs is the kingdom of heaven." They may not be rewarded in this life, but they will be rewarded in the life to come.

The word *persecution* is a strong word; it is the same word that is used of a hunter who is going out to hunt rabbits or other game. The Christian is hunted because he is righteous. Christians were being hunted down when Matthew wrote this book. They needed encouragement. Matthew recalled these sayings of Jesus and told them, "Even if you are hunted down for righteousness' sake, your reward will be in heaven."

"Blessed are ye when men shall reproach you, and persecute you, and say all manner of evil against you falsely, for my sake." "Rejoice," he told them as they were being reviled, reproached, and persecuted. Sometimes persecution can be strong even though our lives are not physically threatened. We may be threatened in other ways. Young people are laughed at because they will not do what other young people are doing. Being laughed at is indeed strong persecution. Physical persecution is sometimes not any harder to bear than an attack on a person's ego. But even though persecution is strong, "Rejoice, and be exceeding glad." It is possible to have happiness even when things are going wrong. The peace of God that passes all understanding will be with you if you endure. "Rejoice, and be exceeding glad, for great is your reward in heaven." One day we are going to stand and be honored in heaven because we have been strong as Christians. We have stood up for the right; we have been faithful as Christians.

Why should we rejoice? For one thing we know that we have a reward coming in heaven. The fact that we are being persecuted for righteousness' sake shows that we are standing for something. We ought to be glad that we are strong enough to stand up for Christ. This should give us a sense of accomplishment! Jesus continued by saying that they persecuted "the prophets who were before you." He is saying that we are in the company of all the great prophets who have gone before us. Abraham was persecuted; Elijah was persecuted; Isaiah, according to church tradition, was "sawn asunder" with a sword. Other great men such as Amos and John the Baptist were persecuted. We are in the company of great people when we are being persecuted for righteousness' sake. Standing for Christ should make us feel glad. And what can compare with the rewards he has promised to those who endure to the end?

QUESTIONS FOR DISCUSSION

1. How would you define the word "personality"?
2. What do the scriptures say about personality?
3. If we were all real Christians, how would this affect our personalities?
4. In what ways are you the same as you were when you were 10 years old?

5. In what ways are you different?
6. What kind of child-rearing practices produce healthy personalities?
7. Discuss scriptures that have helped you to change.

13

The Joys of Being a Christian

"Rejoice in the Lord always; again I will say, Rejoice" (Phil. 4:4). This remarkable statement was made by the apostle Paul while he was in prison. He could make his supplication with joy (Phil. 1:4); proclaim Christ with continued rejoicing (Phil. 1:18); rejoice even if offered as a sacrifice (Phil. 2:17); and could ask others who were being persecuted to rejoice in the Lord with him (Phil. 2:8, 3:1). This same apostle emphasized joy as a fruit of the Spirit (Gal. 5:22) and states that "the kingdom of God is not eating and drinking, but righteousness and peace and joy in the Holy Spirit" (Rom. 14:17).

The message of the Bible is a message that can bring joy to those who really listen. This can be illustrated by a portion of Scripture from the apostle Peter, as recorded in I Peter 1:5-11. Christians rejoiced because of the promise of salvation. They rejoiced even while suffering, which proved their faith to be more precious than gold tried by fire. Through their faith in one whom they had not seen, they rejoiced with joy unspeakable because they knew that the result of their faith was the salvation of their souls. This joy and faith is possible because of the grace of God, which was related by the great prophets of God. They not only foretold the sufferings of Christ but also the glories that should follow them.

Joy is deeper than happiness. Happiness is a natural result of the external conditions of one's life; joy springs from deep within a person's inner being, from a stream that continues to run though circumstances are adverse. Joy is possible even without good health, friendly neighbors, or favorable circumstances. Joy can exist with sorrow. Although Jesus was a man of sorrows (Isa. 53:3), he also pressed forward to do God's will

121

because of the joy that was before him (Heb. 12:2). Paul and Silas could sing praises to God while in prison (Acts 16:23–33). Such joy is hard to express, as indicated by Shakespeare when he said: "Silence is the perfectest herald of joy; I were but little happy if I could say how much." Such joy, found deep within, springs from deep convictions, from God and from Christ Jesus, our Lord.

The beatitudes of Matthew 5 indicate that real Christian happiness comes from being a certain kind of person. Blessed is the man who can leave himself and take on divine characteristics. Therefore, it is no surprise that on the birthday of the church (Acts 2) her first members took their food with gladness. The apostles, though physically abused, rejoiced that they were counted worthy to suffer dishonor for the name of Christ (Acts 5:41). And the Eunuch, having obeyed the gospel, could go on his way rejoicing (Acts 8:39). Joy is inherent in Christianity.

The Joy of a Clear Conscience

One of the greatest joys of the Christian is the joy of a clear conscience. There is joy in the knowledge of being cleansed by the blood of Christ (I John 1:7). It is a wonderful feeling to know that one's sins have been forgiven (Acts 2:38). What a burden it is to carry a load of sin on one's heart! Christ came to take away that burden! Without forgiveness there can be no eternal joy.

The value of forgiveness is illustrated many times in the Bible. Because of his inquisition against Christians, Paul's burden of guilt was heavy; yet he was able to speak of the peace of God which passes all understanding (Phil. 4:7). His conscience was clear; therefore, he had peace.

A picture of David's internal makeup before forgiveness is one of turmoil, anguish, fear, and apprehension because of his sin (Ps. 51). Yet in this same psalm he speaks of the joy which he felt internally because of the refuge and salvation he found in God's forgiveness. He had joy because he had a clear conscience. His clear conscience did not come from a perfect life but from God's forgiveness.

When we were children we were often unhappy because of a guilty conscience. We feared our parents because we knew we had done wrong. But we also experienced the joy of reconciliation when we received forgiveness from our parents.

The Bible illustrates the anguish of one who has a guilty conscience. Jonah felt anguish and fear when he was fleeing from the presence of God. How boxed in and utterly ridiculous he must have felt when he was inside the great fish. Yet he received God's deliverance and forgiveness. With a clear conscience he was able to go and preach God's message to the people of Nineveh.

Cain, on the other hand, was a fugitive and a wanderer all of his days because his conscience was not clear. He reeled and staggered in desperation after he murdered his brother Abel. His despair was not true repentance but regret because of his punishment. Therefore, he did not experience joy but rather alienation through banishment from the presence of God. He dwelt in the land of Nod, the land of wandering. A good conscience causes one to have a sense of unity, of purpose, and of joy in life.

The Bible not only expresses the loneliness and distress that comes to a person because of his sins, but it also reveals God's grace and forgiveness. The message is one of redemption. Peter expresses it this way: "Knowing that ye were redeemed, not with corruptible things, with silver or gold, from your vain manner of life handed down from your father; but with precious blood, as of a lamb without blemish and without spot, even the blood of Christ" (I Peter 1:18–19). This redemption is in the blood of Christ and comes to the person who completely accepts and obeys Christ. Such a person believes (John 3:16), repents (Luke 13:3), confesses his faith in Christ (Rom. 10:9–10), and is immersed into the death of Christ, whose blood was shed to redeem all people from their sins (Rom. 6:3–5). The Ethiopian Eunuch is an illustration of this process. He heard that Jesus was the Messiah of the Old Testament, believed this message, accepted Christ as his sin offering, and was immersed into Jesus (Acts 8). Everything he did was merely his way of accepting the sin offering of God for his sins. He, therefore, had a clear conscience and could go on his way with joy in his heart.

The Joy of Christian Fellowship

Loneliness is one of the major problems of our day. Ask any group of people what their major problems are and loneliness will usually be listed among the top five. Loneliness is possible even in a crowd. Parents feel it when their children leave home, a widow when her husband dies, a widower when his wife dies, divorced people when the divorce is final. Loneliness is real. We feel that others do not understand, that they have their own problems. We feel weak because we stand alone. There seems to be no one who can help.

The Christian is never alone. The Christian has fellowship with God, Christ, and the Holy Spirit (II Cor. 13:13; Rom. 8:9–17). The Christian has fellowship with other Christians. The early church continued in fellowship with one another not only in the worship services of the church but also in the everyday activities of life. Such fellowship with other Christians is a hint of the wonderful fellowship that will come to us when this life is over. Then we will enjoy the blessed fellowship of God, Christ, the Holy Spirit, the angels, and the redeemed of all ages.

Great strength comes from fellowship with other Christians in this life. When we feel weak, others may be strong and can help if we will only let them. We can do all things through Christ who strengthens us (Phil. 4:13). We can be strengthened in the grace that is in Christ Jesus (II Tim. 2:2). Fear can be dispelled because God is the strength of our life. "Of whom shall I be afraid?" (Ps. 27:1). God can become our refuge and strength, a very present help in trouble (Ps. 46:1). Such strength is needed by everyone. The apostle Paul, though one of the greatest men in history, is a good illustration of one who still needed strength. He accepted strength from God, from Christ, from the Holy Spirit, and from his associates (II Cor. 2:13). He came to know that when he was weak, then he was strong (II Cor. 12). This reliance on fellowship became the secret of Paul's power and effectiveness. His joy was perfected and multiplied because it was shared.

The Joy of Leading Others to Christ

A Christian will try to lead others to Christ because he has been commanded to do so. He knows that Jesus has told him to go into all the world and preach the gospel to every creature (Mark 16:15). He realizes that he may not be required to move to another location himself, but that he is required to do what he can to spread the gospel.

Perhaps an even greater motivation for leading others to

Christ is that doing so brings real joy. Parents who have helped lead their children to Christ know this joy. What a thrill it is to see a child accept Christ, to know of his joy and of his relationship with God! Ministers and missionaries know this feeling when they see someone accept Christ. What a wonderful feeling of joy to lead others to Christ!

One young college student went on a campaign with his college group to a large state university. This campaign was held during the spring break. He sacrificed his spring vacation in order to lead others to Christ. His group was able to baptize four people and teach seven hundred others during those few days. Although they had never tried to lead others to Christ before, they were very surprised at what a wonderful feeling they had because of the experience of bringing people to Christ. One student expressed it this way, "Man, I was thrilled." Another said, "Then, I had the greatest feeling and the greatest joy of my life. I knew that God was working through me." He knew that he was working hand in hand with God. He knew that he was leading them to the peace of God which passes all understanding.

The Joy of Pleasing Our Father

There is not only great joy for the Christian in having a clear conscience, in Christian fellowship, and in leading others to Christ, but there is also joy in the knowledge of pleasing God. This joy can only come to one who has a deep conviction that God rewards those who diligently seek him. It comes from a knowledge of God's pleasure in obedience and displeasure in disobedience.

Such joy can be well illustrated by the parent–child relationship. Who does not remember the pleased feeling that comes from having been obedient to his parents? If you know what they want you to do, and you do it, you have a pleased feeling because of your love for them. A person whose parents want him to become a Christian feels pleased when he becomes one because he knows that he has pleased his parents. Likewise, he knows that he has pleased God, and this is even more important. The young boy who knows that his parents value the preaching of the gospel feels good when he becomes a preacher of the gospel because he knows he has pleased his parents as well as God. What father has not experienced pleasure at the obedience of his children? What child has not looked at his father's face to find out if he is pleased when he wins an athletic contest, when he learns his Bible lesson, or when he brings home a good report card from school?

Likewise, it is joy unspeakable to please our Father in heaven. How triumphant and wonderful it will be to hear him say, "Well done thou good and faithful servant." Even when times are rough, a Christian can continue to pattern his lifestyle after Jesus because he knows that in doing so he is pleasing his Father. This brings great joy because he knows he is living hand in hand with God, that his life has purpose, and that his work is not in vain (I Cor. 15:58).

Blessed is the person who is not self-centered but whose character is centered in Jesus. Blessed is the person who experiences real forgiveness through the blood of Jesus. Blessed is the person who has a clear conscience, the person who experiences real Christian fellowship, the person who leads others to Christ, and the person who pleases his Father. Real joy comes to such a person. He can sing the message of Christianity, "Joy to the world, the Lord has come. Let earth receive her King."

QUESTIONS FOR DISCUSSION

1. How would you define joy?
2. What produces Christian joy in your life?
3. Do you ever lose it? What causes you to lose it?
4. What can you do to get it back?
5. Is it possible to have a clear conscience all of the time?
6. What does personality have to do with joy?
7. Discuss the statement: "Christ died for our sins, not for our happiness." Is salvation and happiness a true dicotomy or a false dicotomy?

For Further Reading

Bahnsen, Greg L. *Homosexuality: A Biblical View.* Grand Rapids: Baker Book House, 1978.

Baxter, Batsell Barrett. *When Life Tumbles In.* Grand Rapids: Baker Book House, 1974.

Collins, Gary R. *The Rebuilding of Psychology.* Wheaton, Illinois: Tyndale House Publishers, 1977.

Crabb, Lawrence J., Jr. *Basic Principles of Biblical Counseling.* Grand Rapids: Zondervan Publishing House, 1975.

Dobson, James. *Some Things Wives Wish Their Husbands Knew About Women.* Wheaton, Illinois: Tyndale House Publishers, 1978.

Haggai, John Edmund. *How to Win Over Worry.* Grand Rapids: Zondervan Publishing House, 1959.

Harris, T. A. *I'M OK, You're OK.* New York: Harper and Row, 1969.

Jerkins, E. Ray. *Taking Time for Marriage.* Nashville: Gospel Advocate, 1977.

Kreis, Bernadine and Pattie, Alice. *Up from Grief.* New York: The Seabury Press, 1969.

LaHaye, Tim. *Understanding the Male Temperament.* Old Tappan, New Jersey: Fleming H. Revell, 1975.

LaHaye, Tim and LaHaye, Beverly. *The Act of Marriage.* Grand Rapids: Zondervan Publishing House, 1976.

Larsen, Dale. *The Christian Home.* Austin: R. B. Sweet, 1963.

Leach, Max. *Christianity and Mental Health.* Dubuque: Wm. C. Brown, 1957.

Lewin, S. A. and Gilmore, John. *Sex Without Fear.* Scotch Plains, New Jersey: Medical Research Press, 1950.

Maslow, A. H. *Motivation and Personality.* New York: Harper, 1954.

Miles, Herbert J. *Sexual Happiness in Marriage.* Grand Rapids: Zondervan Publishing House, 1967.

Minirth, Frank B. and Meier, Paul D. *Happiness Is a Choice.* Grand Rapids: Baker Book House, 1978.

Narramore, Clyde M. *A Christian View of Birth Control.* Grand Rapids: Zondervan Publishing House, 1961.

———. *How to Win Over Nervousness*. Grand Rapids: Zondervan Publishing House, 1969.

Sall, Millard J. *Faith, Psychology and Christian Maturity*. Grand Rapids: Zondervan Publishing House, 1975.

Thomas, J. D. *Divorce and Remarriage*. Abilene: Biblical Research Press, 1977.

Warren, Thomas B., ed. *Your Marriage Can Be Great*. Jonesboro, Arkansas: National Christian Press, 1978.

Printed in the United States
127969LV00002B/31-45/A